Strengthen My Spirit

© 2011 by Barbour Publishing, Inc.

Print ISBN 978-1-61626-969-2

eBook Editions:
Adobe Digital Edition (.epub) 978-1-62029-454-3
Kindle and MobiPocket Edition (.prc) 978-1-62029-453-6

Scripture quotations marked KJV are taken from the King James Version of the Bible.

Scripture quotations marked NKJV are taken from the New King James Version®. Copyright © 1982 by Thomas Nelson, Inc. Used by permission. All rights reserved.

Scripture quotations marked NIV are taken from the HOLY BIBLE, NEW INTERNATIONAL VERSION®. NIV®. Copyright © 1973, 1978, 1984 by International Bible Society. Used by permission of Zondervan. All rights reserved.

Scripture quotations marked NASB are taken from the New American Standard Bible, © 1960, 1962, 1963, 1968, 1971, 1972, 1973, 1975, 1977, 1995 by The Lockman Foundation. Used by permission.

Italics have been added for emphasis in many scripture passages at the beginning of readings.

Published by Barbour Publishing, Inc., P.O. Box 719, Uhrichsville, Ohio 44683, www.barbourbooks.com

Our mission is to publish and distribute inspirational products offering exceptional value and biblical encouragement to the masses.

 Member of the
Evangelical Christian
Publishers Association

Printed in the United States of America.

Strengthen My Spirit

CHARLES
SPURGEON

BARBOUR
PUBLISHING

INTRODUCTION

Charles Spurgeon is considered the most widely read preacher in history, excluding those of the Bible. Throughout his lifetime, he preached to over ten million people.

This godly pastor was well acquainted with hardship. He endured personal and family illness, as well as the enormous task of leading a church whose congregation faced numerous difficulties. Spurgeon did not merely instruct his listeners to ask God for the power to withstand adversity, however; he was a living testimony of one who relied on God to be his strength.

Strengthen My Spirit is a compilation of lightly edited selections from Spurgeon's sermons and writings, preceded by brief passages of scripture. We pray that his words encourage you to deepen your relationship with Christ. You may be experiencing hardships: financial distress, a broken relationship, physical illness. . . . Whatever you are facing, God longs to hear you call out, "Lord, strengthen my spirit."

*I pray that out of his glorious riches
he may strengthen you with power through his Spirit
in your inner being, so that Christ may dwell
in your hearts through faith.*

EPHESIANS 3:16–17 NIV

New Heart

"I will give you a new heart and put a new spirit in you."

Ezekiel 36:26 NIV

"Behold," says Christ, "I make all things new." What a wonder it is that a man should ever have a new heart!

You know if a lobster loses its claw in a fight it can get a new claw, and that is thought to be very marvelous. It would be very wonderful if men should be able to grow new arms and new legs, but who ever heard of a creature that grew a new heart?

You may have seen a bough lopped off a tree, and you may have thought that perhaps the tree will sprout again and there will be a new limb, but who ever heard of old trees getting new sap and a new core?

But my Lord and Master, the crucified and exalted Savior, has given new hearts and new cores; He has put the vital substance into man afresh and made new creatures of them. I am glad to notice the tear in your eye when you think on the past, but wipe it away now, and look up to the cross and say—

Just as I am, without one plea,
But that Your blood was shed for me,
And that You bid'st me come to You,
O Lamb, O God, I come.

"Make me a new creature!" If you have said that from your heart, you are a new creature, dear brother, and we will rejoice together in this regenerating Savior.

CHRIST'S PRAYER FOR HIS CHILDREN

I pray not that thou shouldest take them out of the world,
but that thou shouldest keep them from the evil.

JOHN 17:15 KJV

This prayer of Christ is an ever-precious portion to all true believers, from the fact that each of them has an inalienable interest in it.

Every one of us, beloved, when we listen to the words of Christ should recollect that He is praying for us; that while it is for the great body of His elect He intercedes in this chapter and the one preceding it, yet it is also for each believer in particular that He offers intercession.

However weak we are, however poor, however little our faith, or however small our grace may be, our names are still written on His heart; nor shall we lose our share in Jesus' love.

Oh, poor sinner, do not be doubtful of my Master's power. Do but touch the hem of His garment, and you shall be made whole. Like the poor woman in the crowd, get at it and touch it, and He will surely say unto you, "You are saved." If you will go to Him with this cry,

> *I'm a poor sinner and nothing at all,*
> *And Jesus Christ is my all in all,*

then you will see the blessed reason why Jesus interceded thus: "I pray not that thou shouldest take them out of the world."

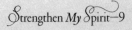

NEVER FORSAKEN

And they that *know thy* name will
put their trust in *thee*: for *thou, Lord,*
hast not forsaken them that seek *thee*.

PSALM 9:10 KJV

Fellowship with Christ is so honorable a thing that it is worthwhile to suffer, that we may thereby enjoy it. You have sometimes heard me express a desire that I might be in the number of those who shall be alive and remain, and so shall escape death; but a dear friend of mine says he had rather die, in order that he might thus have fellowship with Christ in His sufferings, and the thought finds an echo in my own breast.

To die with Jesus makes death a perfect treasure; to be a follower in the grave with Him makes death a pleasure. Moreover you and I might be taken for cowards, although we may have fellowship with Him in His glory, if we had no scars to prove the sufferings we had passed through and the wounds we had received for His name.

Thus again you see it is for our good to be here; we should not have known fellowship with the Savior if we had not stayed here a little while. I should never have known the Savior's love half as much if I had not been in the storms of affliction.

How sweet it is to learn the Savior's love when nobody else loves us! When friends flee, what a blessed thing it is to see that the Savior does not forsake us but still keeps us and holds us fast and clings to us and will not let us go! Oh, beloved brother and sister, believe that your remaining here on earth is for your eternal benefit.

A CALL TO WIN SOULS

The fruit of the righteous is a tree of life,
and he who wins souls is wise.

PROVERBS 11:30 NKJV

Why is it that saints do not die as soon as they are converted? Because God meant that they should be the means of the salvation of their brethren. You would not surely wish to go out of the world if there were a soul to be saved by you. If I could go to glory before I had converted all the souls allotted to me, I should not be happy. We do not wish to enter heaven until our work is done, for it would make us uneasy if there were one single soul left to be saved by our means.

Tarry then, Christian; there is a sinner to be saved from his sins, a rebel to be turned from the error of his ways, and perhaps that sinner is one of your relatives. Perhaps you are spared in this world because there is a wayward son of yours not yet saved, and God has designed to make you the favored instrument of bringing him to glory. It may be that you are kept here because one of your offspring, by your instrumentality, is yet to be saved. Tarry then for your son's sake. I know how deeply you love him, and for his sake, surely, you are content to be left here a little while, counting it for the best that you may bring in your son to glory with you.

Enduring Trials
for God's Glory

Now for a little while you may have had to suffer grief in
all kinds of trials. These have come so that your faith–
of greater worth than gold, which perishes even though refined
by fire–may be proved genuine and may result in praise,
glory and honor when Jesus Christ is revealed.

1 Peter 1:6–7 niv

A tried saint brings more glory to God than an untried one.
I think in my own soul that a believer in a prison reflects
more glory on his Master than a believer in paradise, that
a child of God in the burning, fiery furnace, whose hair is
yet unscorched and upon whom the smell of the fire has not
passed, displays more the glory of the Godhead than even he
who stands with a crown upon his head, perpetually singing
praises before the Father's throne.

Nothing reflects so much honor on a workman as a trial
of his work and its endurance of it. So it is with God. It honors
Him when His saints preserve their integrity. Peter honored
Christ more when he walked on the water than when he stood
upon the land. There was no glory given to God by his walking on the solid shore, but there was glory reflected when he
walked on the water.

If we could but add more jewels to the crown of Christ by
remaining here, why should we wish to be taken out of the
world? We should say, "It is blessed to be anywhere where we
can glorify Him."

Blessed by God

Praise be to the *Lord*, to *God* our *Savior*, who daily
bears our burdens. Our *God* is a *God* who *saves*;
from the *Sovereign Lord* comes escape from death.

PSALM 68:19-20 NIV

Are any of you inclined to murmur? Do you think God deals
harshly with you? Well, you are what you are by His grace.
Though you are not what you wish to be, remember you are
not what—if strict justice were carried out—you would be. In
the poorhouse you might be—few admire that residence. In
the prison you might be—God preserves you from the sin that
would bring you there. At the grave's mouth you might be—
on the sickbed, on the verge of eternity. God's holiest saints
have not been spared from the grave.

O God, when we think of what we are not because Your
grace has kept us from it, we can only say, "You have loaded
us with benefits."

Think of what you are, you Christians. You are God's children; you are joint heirs with Christ. The "many mansions"
are for you; the palms and harps of the glorified are for you.
You have a share in all that Christ has and is and shall be. In
all the gifts of His ascension, you have a part; in the gifts that
come to us through His being seated at the right hand of God,
you have your share; and in the glories of the Second Coming,
you shall partake.

See how in the present and in the past and in the future,
He loads you with benefits.

Praise Him!

I will praise Your name forever and ever.

PSALM 145:2 NKJV

The one occupation of a Christian is to praise his God. Now in order to do this, we must maintain by God's grace a grateful, happy, praiseful frame of mind; and we must endeavor to express that condition of mind by songs of gratitude. Let us make both ends of the day bright with His praise, and throughout the day. We are in a wrong state of mind if we are not in a thankful state of mind. There is something wrong with you if you cannot praise God.

"Oh!" a person says. "Even in trouble?" Yes, in every bitter trouble, too, for Job could say, "The Lord gave, and the Lord has taken away, and blessed be the name of the Lord."

"But are we never to be sorrowful?" Yes, yet always rejoicing. How can that be? The Lord will teach you! It is a work of grace. Cast down but yet rejoicing in the Lord! He lifts up the light of His countenance upon us, even when heart and flesh are failing us. There is something amiss when our heart does not praise God.

When your heart is glad, praise Him with your lips. Do you work alone? Sing. Perhaps, if you work with others, you cannot; then sing with your heart. Habitually praise Him. All our actions, as well as our thoughts and words, should praise Him who always blesses us. You may stop praising God when He stops having mercy on you—not until then.

Our Never-Changing God

"For *I* am the *Lord*, *I* do not change;
therefore you are not consumed."

Malachi 3:6 NKJV

What a consolation it is that our God never changes! What He was yesterday, He is today. What we find Him today, we shall find Him forever. Are you struggling against sin? Don't struggle in your own strength: It is God who performs all things for you. Victories over sin are only sham victories unless we overcome through the blood of the Lamb and through the power of divine grace.

May we have what we really think we have—no surface work but deep, inner, spiritual life fashioned in us from God—yes, every good spiritual thing from Him who performs all things for us; and I say, whatever struggles may come, whatever temptations may overwhelm, or whatever thunderclouds may burst over your heads, you shall not be deserted, much less destroyed.

In spiritual things it is God who performs all things for you. Rest in Him then. You cannot work to save your own soul; Christ is the Savior. If He cannot save you, you certainly cannot save yourself. Why do you rest your hopes where hopes never should be rested? Or let me change the question: Why do you fear where you should never have hoped? Instead of fearing that you cannot hold on, fear holding on yourself and never look in that direction again. Let your entire reliance be fixed in Him. Cast the burden of your care on Him who performs all things for you.

BOASTING IN THE LORD

My soul shall make its boast in the *Lord*;
the humble shall hear of it and be glad.

PSALM 34:2 NKJV

Boasting is generally annoying. Even those who boast themselves cannot endure the boasting of other people. But there is one kind of boasting that even the humble can bear to hear—in fact, they are glad to hear it. "The humble shall hear thereof and be glad." That must be boasting in God—a holy glorifying and extolling the Most High with words sought out with care that might magnify His blessed name.

You will never exaggerate when you speak good things of God. It is not possible to do so. Try, dear brethren, and boast in the Lord. There are many poor, trembling, doubting, humble souls who can hardly tell whether they are the Lord's people or not and are half afraid whether they will be delivered in the hour of trouble, who will become comforted when they hear you boasting. "The humble shall hear thereof and be glad."

"Why," says the humble soul, "the God who helped him can help me. He who brought him up through the deep waters and landed him safely can also take me through the river and through the sea and give me final deliverance."

My soul shall make her boast in the Lord. "The humble shall hear thereof and be glad."

NEARER TO GOD

Get thee up into the high mountain.

ISAIAH 40:9 KJV

Each believer should be thirsting for God, for the living God, and longing to climb the hill of the Lord and see Him face-to-face. My soul thirsts of the cup that is reserved for those who reach the mountain's brow and bathe their brows in heaven. How pure are the dews of the hills, how fresh is the mountain air, how rich the fare of the dwellers aloft whose windows look into the New Jerusalem!

Many saints are content to live like men in coal mines who see not the sun; they eat dust like the serpent when they might taste the ambrosial meat of angels, they are content to wear the miner's garb when they might put on the king's robes, and tears mar their faces when they might anoint them with celestial oil. Many a believer pines in a dungeon when he might walk on the palace roof and view the goodly land of Lebanon.

Rouse yourself from your low condition! Cast away your sloth, your lethargy, your coldness, or whatever interferes with your chaste and pure love for Christ, your soul's husband. Make Him the source, the center, and the circumference of all your soul's range of delight.

What charms you into such folly as to remain in a pit when you may sit on a throne? Rest no longer satisfied with your dwarfish attainments, but press forward to things more sublime and heavenly. Aspire to a higher, a nobler, a fuller life. Upward to heaven! Nearer to God!

THE REDEMPTION OF GOD

I will *deliver* thee out of the hand of the wicked,
and *I* will *redeem* thee out of the hand of the terrible.

JEREMIAH 15:21 KJV

Note the glorious personality of the promise. "I will"—the Lord Jehovah Himself interposes to deliver and redeem His people. He pledges Himself personally to rescue them. His own arm will do it that He may have the glory.

There is not a word said of any effort of our own that may be needed to assist the Lord. Neither our strength nor our weakness is taken into the account, but the lone I, like the sun in the heavens, shines out resplendent in all-sufficiency. Peace, you unbelieving thoughts—be still and know that the Lord reigns.

Nor is there a hint concerning secondary means and causes. The Lord says nothing of friends and helpers: He undertakes the work alone and feels no need of human arms to aid Him. Vain are all our lookings around to companions and relatives; they are broken reeds if we lean upon them—often unwilling when able and unable when they are willing. Since the promise comes alone from God, it would be well to wait only upon Him, and when we do so, our expectation never fails us. In all times of fiery trial, in patience let us possess our souls.

Contentment in God

O *fear* the LORD, ye *his* saints: for there is no want
to them that fear *him*. The young lions do lack,
and suffer hunger: but they that seek the LORD
shall not want any good thing.

PSALM 34:9–10 KJV

They are very strong, those young lions. They are fierce. They
are voracious. They are cunning. And yet they do lack and
suffer hunger.

And there are many men in this world who are very clever,
strong in body, and active in mind. They say that they can take
care of themselves, and perhaps they do appear to prosper;
but we know that often those who are the most prosperous
apparently are the most miserable of men. They are young
lions, but they do lack and suffer hunger.

But when a man's soul lives upon God, he may have very
little of this world, but he will be perfectly content. He has
learned the secret of true happiness. He does not want any
good things, for the things that he does not have, he does not
wish to have. He brings his mind down to his estate if he cannot bring his estate to his mind.

He is thankful to have a little spending money, but his
treasure is above. He likes to have the best things last, and so
he is well content, if he has food and raiment, to press on his
way to the rest that remains for the people of God. "The young
lions do lack, and suffer hunger; but they that seek the Lord
shall not want any good thing."

BENEVOLENT FORESIGHT

Thou, O God, hast prepared of
thy goodness for the poor.

PSALM 68:10 KJV

God anticipates our needs, and out of the fullness that He has treasured up in Christ Jesus, He provides of His goodness for the poor. You may trust Him for all the necessities that can occur, for He has infallibly foreknown every one of them. God has marked with prescient eye all the requirements of His poor wandering children, and when those needs occur, supplies are ready. It is goodness that He has prepared for the poor in heart, goodness and goodness only. "My grace is sufficient for thee." "As your days, so shall your strength be."

Is your heart heavy? God knew it would be; the comfort that your heart wants is treasured in the sweet assurance of the text. You are poor and needy, but He has thought of you and has the exact blessing that you require in store for you. Plead the promise, believe it, and obtain its fulfillment.

Do you feel that you never were so consciously vile as you are now? Behold, the crimson fountain is open still with all its former efficacy, to wash your sin away. Never shall you come into such a position that Christ cannot aid you.

No pinch shall ever arrive in your spiritual affairs in which Jesus Christ shall not be equal to the emergency, for your history has all been foreknown and provided for in Jesus.

WAIT FOR THE LORD

Therefore will the *LORD* wait,
that *he* may be gracious unto you.

ISAIAH 30:18 KJV

God often delays in answering prayer. If you have been knocking at the gate of mercy and have received no answer, shall I tell you why the mighty Maker has not opened the door and let you in? Our Father has reasons known only to Himself.

Sometimes it is to show His power and His sovereignty, that men may know that Jehovah has a right to give or to withhold. More frequently the delay is for our profit. Perhaps you are kept waiting in order that your desires may be more fervent. God knows that delay will quicken and increase desire, and that if He keeps you waiting, you will see your necessity more clearly and will seek more earnestly; and that you will prize the mercy all the more for its long tarrying.

There may also be something in you that needs to be removed before the joy of the Lord is given. Perhaps you may be placing some little reliance on yourself instead of trusting entirely to the Lord Jesus.

Your prayers are all filed in heaven; and if not immediately answered, they are certainly not forgotten, but in a little while shall be fulfilled to your delight and satisfaction. Let not despair make you silent, but continue constantly in earnest supplication.

ASSURANCE OF GOD'S FAITHFULNESS

The one who calls you is faithful and he will do it.

1 THESSALONIANS 5:24 NIV

Heaven is a place where we shall never sin; there will be no tempter to ensnare our feet. There the wicked cease from troubling and the weary are at rest. Heaven is the "undefiled inheritance"; it is the land of perfect holiness, and therefore of complete security.

But do not the saints even on earth sometimes taste the joys of blissful security? The doctrine of God's Word is that all who are in union with the Lamb are safe, that all the righteous shall hold on their way, that those who have committed their souls to the keeping of Christ shall find Him a faithful and immutable preserver.

Sustained by such a doctrine we can enjoy security even on earth; not that high and glorious security that renders us free from every slip, but that holy security that arises from the sure promise of Jesus that none who believe in Him shall ever perish but shall be with Him where He is. Let us often reflect with joy on the doctrine of the perseverance of the saints and honor the faithfulness of our God by a holy confidence in Him.

Look upon Him as faithful and true, and therefore bound and engaged to present you, the weakest of the family, with all the chosen race before the throne of God. You will have the enjoyments that ravish the souls of the perfect saints above, if you can believe with unstaggering faith that "the one who calls you is faithful and He will do it."

Our Holy Guide

And the *Lord* shall guide thee continually.

ISAIAH 58:11 KJV

"The Lord shall guide thee." Not an angel, but Jehovah shall guide you. God has not left you in your earthly pilgrimage to an angel's guidance: He Himself leads the van. You may not see the cloudy, fiery pillar, but Jehovah will never forsake you.

Notice the word "shall"—"The Lord shall guide thee." How certain this makes it! How sure it is that God will not forsake us! His precious "shalls" and "wills" are better than men's oaths. "I will never leave thee nor forsake thee."

Then observe the adverb "continually." We are not merely to be guided sometimes, but we are to have a perpetual monitor; not occasionally to be left to our own understanding, and so to wander, but we are continually to hear the guiding voice of the Great Shepherd; and if we follow close at His heels, we shall not err, but be led by a right way to a city to dwell in.

If you have to change your position in life, if you have to emigrate to distant shores, if it should happen that you are cast into poverty or uplifted suddenly into a more responsible position than the one you now occupy, if you are thrown among strangers or cast among foes, tremble not, for "the Lord shall guide you continually."

There are no dilemmas out of which you shall not be delivered if you live near to God. He goes not amiss who goes in the company of God. You have infallible wisdom to direct you, immutable love to comfort you, and eternal power to defend you.

GOD'S THOUGHTS
FOR HIS CHILDREN

"I remember you."

JEREMIAH 2:2 NKJV

Let us note that Christ delights to think upon His Church and to look upon her beauty. As the bird returns often to its nest and as the wayfarer hastens to his home, so does the mind continually pursue the object of its choice. We cannot look too often upon that face that we love; we desire always to have our precious things in our sight.

It is even so with our Lord Jesus. From all eternity "His delights were with the sons of men." His thoughts rolled onward to the time when His elect should be born into the world; He viewed them in the mirror of His foreknowledge. "In your book," He says, "all my members were written, which in continuance were fashioned when as yet there was none of them." When the world was set upon its pillars, He was there, and He set the bounds of the people according to the number of the children of Israel.

As the breastplate containing the names of the tribes of Israel was the most brilliant ornament worn by the high priest, so the names of Christ's elect were His most precious jewels and glittered on His heart. We may often forget to meditate upon the perfections of our Lord, but He never ceases to remember us.

Let us chide ourselves for past forgetfulness and pray for grace ever to bear Him in fondest remembrance. Lord, paint upon the eyeballs of my soul the image of Your Son.

Our Ultimate Inheritance

He will choose our inheritance for us.

Believer, if your inheritance is a lowly one, you should be satisfied with your earthly portion, for you may rest assured that it is the fittest for you. Unerring wisdom ordained your lot and selected for you the safest and best condition.

A large ship is to be brought up the river; now in one part of the stream there is a sandbank. Should someone ask, "Why does the captain steer through the deep part of the channel and deviate so much from a straight line?" his answer would be, "Because I could not get my vessel into harbor at all if I did not keep to the deep channel." So, it may be, you would run aground and suffer shipwreck if your divine Captain did not steer you into the depths of affliction where waves of trouble follow each other in quick succession.

Some plants die if they have too much sunshine. It may be that you are planted where you get but little; you are put there by the loving Husbandman because only in that situation will you bring forth fruit unto perfection. Had any other condition been better for you than the one in which you are, divine love would have put you there. You are placed by God in the most suitable circumstances.

Take up your own daily cross; it is the burden best suited for your shoulder and will prove most effective to make you perfect in every good word and work to the glory of God.

The Compassion of Christ

But *He*, being full of compassion,
forgave their iniquity.

PSALM 78:38 NKJV

Though your sin may have ruined you, Christ can enrich you with better riches. He has compassion. "They will pass by me," you say, "and if they see me in the street, they will not speak to me—even Christians will not." Perhaps that may be, but better than other Christians, tenderer by far, is Jesus.

Is there someone with whom one would associate would be a scandal from which the pure and pious would shrink? The holy, harmless, undefiled one will not disdain even him—for this man receives sinners—He is a friend of sinners. He is never happier than when He is relieving and retrieving the forlorn, the abject, and the outcast. He does not condemn any who confess their sins and seek His mercy.

No pride nestles in His dear heart, no sarcastic word rolls off His gracious tongue, no bitter expression falls from His blessed lips. He still receives the guilty. Pray to Him now; let the silent prayer go up: "My Savior, have pity upon me; be moved with compassion toward me, for if misery be any qualification for mercy, I am a fit object for your compassion."

THE PRESENCE OF GOD

Lo, *I* am with you always.

MATTHEW 28:20 KJV

The Lord Jesus is in the midst of His Church. Not physically, but still in real truth, Jesus is with us. And a blessed truth it is, for where Jesus is, love becomes inflamed. Of all the things in the world that can set the heart burning, there is nothing like the presence of Jesus! A glimpse of Him so overcomes us that we are ready to say, "Turn away Your eyes from me for they have overcome me."

If we know that Jesus is with us, every power will be developed and every grace will be strengthened, and we shall cast ourselves into the Lord's service with heart and soul and strength; therefore is the presence of Christ to be desired above all things.

His presence will be most realized by those who are most like Him. If you desire to see Christ, you must grow in conformity to Him. Bring yourself, by the power of the Spirit, into union with Christ's desires and motives and plans of action, and you are likely to be favored with His company.

Remember His presence may be had. His promise is as true as ever. He delights to be with us. If He does not come, it is because we hinder Him by our indifference. He will reveal Himself to our earnest prayers and graciously suffer Himself to be detained by our entreaties and by our tears, for these are the golden chains that bind Jesus to His people.

PERSEVERE!

Because *I live*, ye shall live also.

JOHN 14:19 KJV

When we once get spiritual life into us, what a thousand enemies there are who try to put it out! Temptation after temptation have I endured until it appeared I must yield my hold on Christ and give up my hope. There has been conflict upon conflict and struggle upon struggle until at last the enemy has gotten his foot upon my neck, and my whole being has trembled; and had it not been for Christ's promise "Because I live, you shall live also," it might have been more difficult for me, and I might have despaired and given up all hope and lay down to die.

The assurance, then, that the spiritual life of the Christian must be maintained because Christ lives, was the only power to get me the victory. Let it teach us, then, this practical lesson: Whenever our spiritual life is very weak and we want it to grow stronger, let us get to the living Christ for the supply of His strength. When you feel you are ready to die spiritually, go to the Savior for revived life.

The text is like a hand that points us to the storehouse. You who are in the desert, there is a secret spring under your feet and you know not where it is; this is the mysterious finger that points you to the spot. Contemplate Christ, believe in Christ, draw yourselves by faith nearer and nearer to the Lord Jesus Christ, and so shall your life receive a divine impetus, which it has not known for many a day.

A Sinner's Repentance

Deliver me from bloodguiltiness, O *God*,
thou *God* of my salvation: and my tongue
shall sing aloud of *thy* righteousness.

PSALM 51:14 KJV

I like that confession and that prayer of David. He does not mince words for he had guiltily caused the blood of Uriah to be shed, and here he admits it with great shame, but with equal honesty and truthfulness. As long as you and I call our sins by pretty names, they will not be forgiven. The Lord knows exactly what your sin is; therefore, do not try to use polite terms for it. Tell Him what it is, so that He knows that you know what it is. "Deliver me from bloodguiltiness, O God, thou God of my salvation."

"But certainly," one may say, "there is no one in the church who needs to pray that prayer." Well, there is one who often feels that he has the need to pray it; for what will happen if I preach not the Gospel, or if I do not preach it with all my heart? It may be that the blood of souls shall be required at my hands.

And, my brothers and sisters, if anything in your example should lead others into sin, or if the neglect of any opportunities that are presented to you should lead others to continue in their sin until they perish, could the sin of bloodguiltiness not be possible for you?

"'Deliver me from bloodguiltiness, O God, thou God of my salvation.' And then, O Lord, when I am forgiven of that, 'my tongue shall sing aloud of your righteousness.'"

A Promise of Hope

But if we *hope* for what we do not yet have,
we *wait* for it patiently.

ROMANS 8:25 NIV

We are expecting that, one of these days, if the chariot and horses of fire do not stop at our door, our dear Lord and Savior will fulfill His promise to us: "If I go and prepare a place for you, I will come again and receive you unto Myself; that where I am, there you may be also."

To a true believer in Jesus, the thought of departing from this world and going to be "forever with the Lord" has no gloom associated with it. Heaven is our home. We are longing for the great reunion with our beloved Lord, from whom we shall then never again be separated. I cannot attempt to depict the scene when He will introduce us to the principalities and powers in heavenly places and invite us to sit with Him. Surely then the holy angels, who have never sinned, will unite in exclaiming, "Behold how He loved them!"

It is a most blessed thought, to my mind, that we may be up there before the hands of that clock complete another round; and if not that soon, it will not be long before all of us who love the Lord will be with Him where He is, and then the last among us shall know more of His love than the greatest of us can ever know while here below.

PERSISTENT PRAYER

And he said, I *beseech thee,*
shew me *thy* glory.

EXODUS 33:18 KJV

Refer to the thirteenth verse of this chapter, where Moses speaks to God: "Now therefore, I pray thee, if I have found grace in your sight, shew me now your way." Moses asked a lesser favor before he requested the greater. He asked to see God's way before he prayed to see His glory.

This is the true manner of prayer. Do not be content with past answers, but double your request and ask again. Nothing pleases God as much as when a sinner comes again with twice as large a petition: "Lord, You heard me last time, and now I come again." Faith is a mighty grace and always grows upon that which it feeds. When God has heard prayer for one thing, faith comes and asks for two things, and when God has given those two things, faith asks for six.

Faith can scale the walls of heaven. She is a giant grace. She takes mountains by their roots and puts them on other mountains and so climbs to the throne in confidence with large petitions, knowing that she shall not be refused. Most of us are too slow to go to God. If we have been heard once, we go away instead of coming again and again, and each time with a larger prayer.

Make your petitions longer and longer. Ask for ten, and if God gives them, then for a thousand, and keep going on until at last you will have enough faith to ask as great a favor as Moses did, "I beseech you, show me your glory."

GOD'S GRACE

Where sin abounded,
grace did much more abound.

ROMANS 5:20 KJV

The only counterforce against sin is grace. And what is grace? Grace is the free favor of God, the undeserved bounty of the ever-gracious Creator against whom we have sinned, the generous pardon, the infinite, spontaneous loving-kindness of the God who has been provoked and angered by our sin; but who, delighting in mercy and grieving to smite the creatures whom He has made, is always ready to pass by transgression, iniquity, and sin, and to save His people from all the evil consequences of their guilt.

Here is a force that is fully equal to the requirements of the duel with sin; for this grace is divine grace, and thus it is omnipotent, immortal, and immutable. This favor of God never changes, and when once it purposes to bless anyone, bless him it will, and none can revoke the blessing.

The gracious purpose of God's free favor to an undeserving man is more than a match for that man's sin, for it brings to bear upon his sin the blood of the incarnate Son of God, and the majestic and mysterious fire of the eternal Spirit who burns up evil and utterly consumes it. With God the Father, God the Son, and God the Holy Spirit united against sin, the everlasting purposes of grace are bound to be accomplished, and sin must be overcome.

SINNERS MADE CLEAN

"I will *cleanse* them from all their iniquity by which they have
sinned against Me, and *I* will *pardon* all
their iniquities by which they have sinned and by
which they have transgressed against Me."

JEREMIAH 33:8 NKJV

It is very wonderful, but it is certainly true, that there are
many persons in heaven in whom sin once abounded. In the
judgment of their fellowmen, some of them were worse sinners than others. There was Saul of Tarsus, there was the dying
thief, there was the woman in the city who was a sinner—a
sinner in a very open and terrible sense.

These, and many more of whom we read in the scriptures,
were all great sinners, and it was a great wonder of grace in
every instance that they should be forgiven; but did they make
poor Christians when they were converted?

Quite the reverse: They loved much because they had
been forgiven much. Among the best servants of God are
many of those who were once the best servants of the devil.
Sin abounded in them, but grace much more abounded when
it took possession of their hearts and lives. They were long
led captive by the devil at his will, but they were never such
servants to Satan as they afterward became to the living and
true God. They threw all the fervor of their intense natures
into the service of their Savior and so rose superior to some of
their fellow disciples, who did not fully realize how much they
owed to their Lord.

SIN AND GRACE

And when *he saw* their faith, *he* said unto him,
Man, thy sins are forgiven thee.

LUKE 5:20 KJV

Sin has brought us very low, but Christ has lifted us higher than we stood before sin cast us down. Sin took away from man his love to God, but Christ has given us a more intense love for God than Adam ever had; for we love God because He has first loved us and given His Son to die for us, and we have, in His greater grace, a good reason for yielding to Him a greater love.

Sin took away obedience from man, but now saints obey to a yet higher degree than they could have done before, for I suppose it would not have been possible for unfallen man to suffer, but now we are capable of suffering for Christ; and many martyrs have gone singing to death for the truth because, while sin made them capable of suffering, Christ's grace has made them capable of obedience to Him in the suffering, and in so doing more prove their allegiance to God than would have been possible if they had never fallen.

Sin has shut us out of Eden; yet let us not weep, for Christ has prepared a better paradise for us in heaven. God has provided for us "a pure river of water of life" and a lovelier garden than Eden ever was; and there we shall forever dwell through the abounding grace of our Lord and Savior Jesus Christ, which has abounded even over our abounding sin.

LISTENING TO THE VOICE OF GOD

"He who is of God hears God's words."

JOHN 8:47 NKJV

Why is it that you are able to confide in God's Word? Surely it is because you know that for God to speak is for Him to do as He has said. By His Word, He made the heavens and the earth, and it is by His Word that the heavens and the earth continue as they are to this day.

God's speaking is very different from man's. Very often, man talks about something that he says he will do, but when he has talked about it, there is an end of the matter as far as he is concerned. Man has spoken, yes, but you can never be sure that with the talking tongue will go the working hand. He who is quick to promise is not always so prompt to perform.

We have many proverbs that remind us that men make light of one another's promises, and well they may; but we must never make light of the promises of God. "He spake, and it was done; he commanded, and it stood fast." So if there is a promise of God to help you in a time of trouble or to preserve you in the hour of temptation or to deliver you out of trial or to give you grace according to your day, that promise is as good as if it had been already performed, since God's Word shall certainly be followed by the fulfillment of it in due season.

CLOSENESS WITH CHRIST

There *I* will *meet* with thee, and *I* will *commune*
with thee from above the mercy seat.

EXODUS 25:22 KJV

It should be our earnest aim to keep unbroken our communion with heaven, for it is the most refreshing thing beneath the sun. This world is like an arid desert where there is no water except as we maintain our communion with Christ.

As long as I can say that the Lord is mine, all things here below are of small account; but if I once doubt that and if I cease to walk with God, then what is there here below that can content my immortal spirit? Without Christ, this world is to us as thorns without the roses and as bitters without the sweets of life. But You, O Lord, make earth to be a heaven to Your saints even when they lie in dungeons, when Your presence cheers them.

It is most important that you maintain your communion with Christ, for that is the only way to keep yourself clear from corruption. And you who have much to do in the church must keep up your communion with Christ, for that is the only way of keeping your service from becoming mechanical and of preventing you from doing good works as a mere matter of routine. You, too, who have much to suffer or even much to enjoy must keep up this holy communion, or else your soul will soon be like a thirsty land where there is no water.

He Will Direct;
We Must Walk

The steps of a good man are ordered by the *Lord*,
and *He delights* in his way.

PSALM 37:23 NKJV

He who walks does not need to think of directing his own steps, for there is One who will direct them for him. What if sin persuades us to take the wrong path and if poor judgment makes us err through oversight? There is no need for us to choose our own fate, but we may bow before the Lord and say, "You shall choose our inheritance for us." The choice is difficult for you; do not choose your own way, but leave it to Him who sees the end from the beginning and who is sure to make the wise choice.

The burden of life is heavy—do not try to carry it, but "cast your burden upon the Lord, and He shall sustain you. Commit your way unto the Lord; trust also in Him, and He shall bring it to pass." Do not let it be your choice; let it be God's choice.

If only we could but once abandon our own choosing and say to the Lord, "Not as I will, but as You will," how much more happy we could be! We should not be troubled by the thought that we should not direct our own steps, but we should be glad becauseour very weakness entitles us to cry to the Lord, "Now that I will not direct my own way, what I do not know, teach me."

KEEP A LOOSE GRASP

*"Lay up for yourselves treasures in heaven. . . .
For where your treasure is, there your
heart will be also."*

MATTHEW 6:20-24 NKJV

Avoid all security as to the present. If you have anything that you prize very highly, hold it very loosely for you may easily lose it. Hold everything earthly with a loose hand, but grasp eternal things with a deathlike grip.

Grasp Christ in the power of the spirit; grasp God, who is your everlasting portion and your unfailing joy. Of everything on earth, it is wise for us to say, "This is not mine to keep." It is essential to say this and to realize that it is true, for everything here is temporary.

Mind what you are doing, you prosperous people, you who have nice homes, you who are investing your money in the funds. There is nothing permanent for you here. Your home is in heaven, your home is not here, and if you find your treasure here, your heart will be here also; but it must not be so. You must keep all earthly treasures out of your heart; let Christ be your treasure, and let Him have your heart.

PERFECT PEACE

Jesus said to the woman,
"Your faith has saved you; *go* in peace."

LUKE 7:50 NIV

When the many tears from her eyes fell upon His feet, He did not withdraw them. When those feet were wiped with the tresses of her hair, still He did not withdraw them; and when she ventured upon a yet closer familiarity and not only kissed His feet but also did not cease to kiss them, He still did not withdraw them but quietly accepted all that she did.

And when the precious ointment was poured in lavish abundance upon those precious feet of His, He did not chastise her; He did not refuse her gifts but tacitly accepted them, although without a word of acknowledgment just then. It is a very blessed thing for any one of you to be accepted before God, even though no word has come from His lips assuring you that you are.

When your tears and cries and secret love and earnest seeking—when your confession of sin, your struggle after faith, and the beginning of your faith—are just accepted by the Lord, although He has not yet said to you, "Your sins are forgiven," it is a very blessed stage for you to have reached; for the Lord does not begin to accept anyone, even by a silence that means consent, and then draw back. He accepted this woman's love and gifts, though, for a time, He gave her no assurance of that acceptance, and that fact must have greatly encouraged her.

Giving Cheerfully

Each man should give what he has decided in
his heart to give, not reluctantly or under
compulsion, for *God loves* a cheerful giver.

2 Corinthians 9:7 niv

That is the most acceptable gift to God that is given rejoicingly. It is well to feel that whatever good your gift may do to the church or the poor or the sick it is twice as much benefit to you to give it.

It is well to give because you love to give: as the flower that pours forth its perfume because it never dreamed of doing otherwise; or like the bird that quivers with song because it is a bird and finds a pleasure in its notes; or like the sun that shines, not by constraint, but because, being a sun, it must shine; or like the waves of the sea that flash back the brilliance of the sun because it is their nature to reflect and not to hoard the light.

Oh, to have such grace in our hearts that we shall joyfully make sacrifices unto our God. The Lord grant that we may have a desire for this; for the bringing of the tithes into the storehouse is the way to the blessing; as the scripture says: "Bring ye all the tithes into the storehouse, that there may be meat in mine house, and prove me now herewith, saith the Lord of hosts, if I will not open you the windows of heaven, and pour you out a blessing, that there shall not be room enough to receive it" (Malachi 3:10 kjv).

STILLNESS OF HEART

"Do not let your heart be troubled,
nor let it be fearful."

JOHN 14:27 NASB

If Christ has saved you, you have the best reason in the world for being the happiest people who ever lived. One man said to another man, who had shared about his salvation, "You should be the happiest man alive."

He answered, "Yes, I am." It was well known that he was very poor. It was said that he did not know where he would get his next meal, but he had eaten the previous meal so he was content to wait for God to provide his next nourishment. He had such simple faith in God that, although he was very poor, he still said he was the happiest man in the world.

Christ has carried your heaviest burdens. He has averted the most terrible disaster that could ever happen to you; the most terrifying calamity you once dreaded can never harm you. You are an heir of God and a joint heir with Jesus Christ. You will have all you really need in this life, and you will have heaven when this life is over.

The Father, the Son, and the Holy Spirit have all united to bless you; and the covenant of peace is signed and sealed and approved, and you will conquer in the end. So, "Let not your heart be troubled; neither let it be afraid."

GOD WILL GRANT RELIEF

God is our refuge and strength,
a very present help in trouble.

PSALM 46:1 KJV

We do not know what we might have been if God's gracious protection had not been like a wall of fire around us, as it still is, for the Lord continues to deliver all those who put their trust in Him. Believe with unquestioning confidence that God is delivering you even now. You know that He has delivered you; be just as sure that He is delivering you at this moment.

"I am locked in a prison of despair." Yes, but your Lord has a key that can open the door and let you out. "But I am in great want," another says. But He knows all about it, and He is going to supply all your needs. Yet another says, "I am sinking in the flood." But he is throwing the life preserver over you. "I am fainting!" says another. But He is putting smelling salts to your nose to refresh your spirit. God is near, ready to revive and encourage your fainting soul.

Perhaps a person says, "I find faith for the past and the ultimate future quite easy, but I don't have enough faith for the present." We sometimes forget that God is "a very present help in trouble," but it is true. He has delivered us, and He will continue to deliver us.

He Has Delivered;
He Will Deliver

He has delivered us from such a deadly peril,
and *he* will deliver us. On *him* we have set our
hope that *he* will continue to deliver us.

2 Corinthians 1:10 niv

There may be many trials before you, but there is an abundance of mercy ready to meet those trials. Troubles that you do not know yet, as well as repetitions of those you have experienced, you will certainly encounter, but the Lord will give you strength and will continue to deliver you.

As the eyes gradually fail and the limbs grow weak and the infirmities of age creep over us, we are likely to be distressed, but our Lord will not forsake us. When severe sickness invades our earthly bodies and our pains multiply and intensify, we wonder how we will endure.

As we consider our death, we wonder how we will be able to bear our last hours. Be encouraged: He who has delivered and does deliver will continue to deliver. Even as the trial comes, the Lord will show you a way of escape.

He has delivered you; give Him your gratitude. He is delivering you; give Him your confidence. He will deliver you; give Him your joy, and begin now to praise Him for mercies that He has yet to show you and for grace that you have not yet experienced but that He will grant you in the future.

God's Unchanging Purpose

For the *Lord Almighty* has purposed, and who can *thwart him?*
His hand is stretched out,
and who can turn it back?

Isaiah 14:27 niv

He is always the same, and everything is always present in His unchanging mind. What was the nature of God when He first determined to deliver me? Was it love? Then it is still love. What was the motive that prompted the Son of God when He came from above and snatched me from the deep waters? It was love, surprising love, and it is surprising love that still moves Him to deliver me.

Did I sing about His faithfulness just the other day? That faithfulness is just the same today. Have I adored His wisdom? That wisdom is not depleted.

There is not only the same nature in God as there always was, but there is also the same unchanging purpose. You and I shift and change, and we do so because we make rash promises and flawed plans; but God, who is infinitely wise, always holds to His purpose. Now if it was His original purpose to save us—and it must have been, or He would never have delivered us as He has done—that purpose still stands and shall stand forever. Though earth fades, though heaven and earth shall pass away, as the morning frost dissolves in the beams of the rising sun, the decree of the immutable Jehovah will never be changed.

Go to God!

Meditate within your heart
on your bed, and be still.

PSALM 4:4 NKJV

There should be special times for meditation. I think everyone should set apart a portion of time every day for this exercise. You may tell me that you have so much to do you cannot make the time for it. I generally take lightly the excuses of those who cannot afford time for obvious responsibilities.

If you do not have the time, you should make it. What time do you get up in the morning? Could you manage to get up fifteen minutes earlier? How long do you take for your dinner? Thirty minutes? Then you read something afterward possibly. Could you spend that time in tranquil communion with your own soul? The Christian will always be lacking if he does not have time for spiritual unity with his God. Those men who know God the best are those who meditate most upon Him.

Do you desire to be strong? Do you wish to be mighty? Do you hope to be valiant for the Lord and useful in His cause? Be careful that you follow the occupation of the psalmist David and meditate. This is a happy occupation.

God Will Sustain

The *Lord* upholdeth all that fall.

PSALM 145:14 KJV

"The Lord upholds all who fall." What a singular expression! How can He hold up those who fall? Yet those who fall, in this sense, are the only persons who stand. It is a remarkable paradox, but it is true. The man who stands on his feet and says, "I am mighty; I am strong enough to stand alone," down he will go; but he who falls into Christ's arms, that man shall not fall.

We may well talk then of Christ's upholding power. Tell it to Christians; tell how He kept you when your feet were going swiftly to hell; how, when fierce temptations did beset you, your Master drove them all away; how, when the enemy was watching, He compassed you with His mighty strength; how, when the arrows fell thickly around you, His mighty arm held the shield before you and so preserved you from them all. Tell how He saved you from death and delivered your feet from falling by making you, first of all, fall down prostrate before Him.

How sweet it is sometimes to talk of God's exalting power after we have been hewed down! How sweet it is to feel God's grace when you have been bowed down! Cannot some of us tell that, when we have been bowed down beneath a load of affliction so that we could not even move, the everlasting arms have been around us and have lifted us up? When Satan has put his foot on our back and we have said, "We shall never be raised up anymore," the Lord has come to our rescue.

Proclaim What He Has Done for You

The eyes of all *look* to *you*, and *you give*
them their food at the proper time.

Psalm 145:15 NIV

We should often speak of how God provides for His creatures in providence. Why should we not tell how God has taken us out of poverty and made us rich, or if He has not done that for us, how He has supplied our wants day by day in an almost miraculous manner!

Have you not sometimes been brought so low, through painful affliction, that you could not rest? And could you not afterward say, "I was brought low, and He helped me." Yes, "I was brought low, and He helped me out of my distress." We have been brought into great straits, but the Lord has delivered us out of them all.

Do not be ashamed to tell the story. Let the world hear that God provides for His people. Go, speak of your Father. Do as the child does who, when he has a little cake given to him, will take it out, and say, "My father gave me this." Do so with all your mercies: Go and tell all the world that you have a good Father, a gracious Father, a heavenly Provider; and though He gives you a small portion, and you only live from hand to mouth, still tell how graciously He gives it and that you would not change your blessed estate for all the world calls good or great.

Talk about Jesus

"Those who have insight will shine brightly
like the brightness of the expanse of heaven,
and those who lead the many to righteousness,
like the stars forever and ever."

Daniel 12:3 NASB

Oh, think of the crowns that are in heaven! So many souls, so many gems! Have you ever thought what it would be to wear in heaven a starless crown? All the saints will have crowns, but those who win souls will have a star in their crown for every soul. Some of you, my friends, will wear a crown without a star; would you like that? You will be happy, you will be blessed, you will be satisfied, I know, when you will be there; but can you bear the thought of never having brought any to Christ?

If you want to win souls, talk about Jesus. There is nothing like talking of Him to lead others to Him. Souls are often converted through godly conversation. Let the praises of Christ always be on your tongue; let Him live on your lips. Speak of Him always; when you walk by the way, when you sit in your house, when you rise up, and even when you lie down. It may be that you have someone to whom it is possible that you may yet whisper the Gospel of the grace of God.

Sing of Christ alone! Christ alone! Christ alone! Jesus, Jesus only! Make Him the theme of your conversation, for "they shall speak of the glory of Your kingdom, and talk of Your power." God give you grace so to do, for Christ's sake!

THE GLORY OF THE LORD

"And the glory of the Lord will be revealed,
and all mankind together will see it."

ISAIAH 40:5 NIV

We anticipate the happy day when the whole world shall be converted to Christ, when kings shall bow down before the Prince of Peace and all nations shall call their Redeemer blessed. We know that the world and all that is in it is one day to be burnt up, and afterward we look for new heavens and for a new earth.

We are not discouraged by the length of His delays; we are not disheartened by the long period that He allots to the Church in which to struggle with little success and much defeat. We believe that God will never suffer this world, which has once seen Christ's blood shed upon it, to be always the devil's stronghold. Christ came to deliver this world from the detested sway of the powers of darkness.

What a shout shall that be when men and angels unite to cry, "Hallelujah, hallelujah, for the Lord God Omnipotent reigneth!" What a satisfaction will it be in that day to have had a share in the fight, to have helped to break the arrows of the bow, and to have aided in winning the victory for our Lord! Happy are they who trust themselves with this conquering Lord and who fight side by side with Him, doing their little in His name and by His strength!

God's Continued Work

By one sacrifice *he* has made perfect
forever those who are being made holy.

HEBREWS 10:14 NIV

If God has made a new creature of man, which is the greatest work of grace, will He not do the lesser work of grace—namely, make the new creature grow up unto perfection? If the Lord has turned you to Himself, never be afraid that He will leave you to perish. If He had meant to destroy you, He would not have done this for you. God does not make creatures for annihilation.

Chemists tell us that though many things are resolved into their primary gases by fire, yet there is not a particle less matter on the earth today than there was when it was created. No spiritual life that comes from God is ever annihilated.

If you have obtained it, it never shall be taken from you—it shall be in you a well of water springing up unto everlasting life. If, when you were an enemy, God looked upon you in grace and changed you and made you what you now are, will He not now that you are reconciled continue to preserve and nurture you until He presents you faultless before His presence with exceeding great joy?

MORE THAN CONQUERORS

In all these things we are more than
conquerors through *him* that *loved* us.

ROMANS 8:37 KJV

A joyous man, such as I have now in my mind's eye, is for all intents and purposes a strong man. He is strong in a calm, restful manner. Whatever happens, he is not ruffled or disturbed. He is not afraid of evil tidings; his heart is fixed, trusting in the Lord.

The ruffled man is ever weak. He is in a hurry and does things poorly. The man full of joy within is quiet; he bides his time and crouches in the fullness of his strength. Such a man, though he is humble, is firm and steadfast. He is not carried away with every wind or bowed by every breeze; he knows what he knows and holds what he holds, and the golden anchor of his hope enters within the veil and holds him fast. His strength is not pretentious but real.

The happiness arising from communion with God breeds in him no boastfulness: He does not talk of what he can do, but he does it; he does not say what he could bear, but he bears all that comes. He does not himself always know what he could do; his weakness is the more apparent to himself because of the strength that the Holy Spirit puts upon him, but when the time comes, his weakness only illustrates the divine might, while the man goes calmly on conquering and to conquer.

THE JOY OF THE LORD

The joy of the *Lord* is your strength.

NEHEMIAH 8:10 KJV

The man who possesses "the joy of the Lord" finds it his strength, in that it fortifies him against temptation. What is there that he can be tempted with? He has more already than the world can offer him as a reward for treachery. He is already rich; who shall snare him with the wages of unrighteousness? He is already satisfied; who is he who can seduce him with pleasing baits?

"Shall such a man as I flee?" The rejoicing Christian is equally proof against persecution. They may well afford to be laughed at who win at such a rate as he does. "You may scoff," he says, "but I know what true religion is within my soul, and your scoffing will not make me relinquish the pearl of great price."

Such a man is, furthermore, made strong to bear affliction; for all the sufferings put upon him are but a few drops of bitterness cast into his cup of bliss, to give a deeper tone to the sweetness that absorbs them.

Such a man becomes strong for service, too. What can he not do who is happy in his God? By his God he leaps over a wall or breaks through a troop. He is strong, too, for any kind of self-sacrifice. To the God who gives him all and remains to him as his perpetual portion, such a man gives up all that he has and does not think it surrender. It is laying up his treasure in his own peculiar treasure-house, even in the God of his salvation.

JESUS ONLY

When they had lifted up their eyes,
they *saw* no one but Jesus only.

MATTHEW 17:8 NKJV

I do desire for my fellow Christians and for myself that more and more the great object of our thoughts, motives, and acts may be "Jesus only." I believe that whenever our religion is most vital it is most full of Christ. Furthermore, when it is most practical, downright, and common sense, it always gets nearest to Jesus. I can bear witness that whenever I am in deeps of sorrow, nothing will do for me but "Jesus only."

I can rest in some degree in the externals of religion, its outward escarpments and bulwarks, when I am in health; but I retreat to the innermost citadel of our holy faith, namely, to the very heart of Christ, when my spirit is assailed by temptation or besieged with sorrow and anguish. What is more, my witness is that whenever I have high spiritual enjoyments—enjoyments right, rare, celestial—they are always connected with Jesus only.

Other religious things may give some kind of joy, and joy that is healthy, too, but the most sublime, the most inebriating, the most divine of all joys must be found in Jesus only.

ACCEPTED IN JESUS

Christ accepted you.

ROMANS 15:7 NIV

I will confess to you that over and over I am myself personally driven to do what I trust you may be led to do today. I look back on my life; and while I have much to thank God for, much in which to see His Spirit's hand, yet when I feel my responsibilities and my shortcomings, my heart sinks within me.

When I think of my transgressions, better known to myself than to anyone else, and remember, too, that they are not known even to me as they are to God, I feel all hope swept away and my soul left in utter despair—until I come anew to the cross and think of who it was who died there, and why He died, and what designs of infinite mercy are answered by His death.

It is so sweet to look up to the Crucified One again and say, "I have nothing but You, my Lord, no confidence but You. If You are not accepted as my substitute, I must perish; if God's appointed Savior is not enough, I have no other. But I know You are the Father's well-beloved and I am accepted in You. You are all I want and all I have."

TRIALS

The trial of your faith. . .

1 PETER 1:7 KJV

Faith untried may be true faith, but it is sure to be little faith, and it is likely to remain dwarfish so long as it is without trials. Faith never prospers so well as when all things are against her: Tempests are her trainers, and lightnings are her illuminators. When a calm reigns on the sea, spread the sails as you will, the ship moves not to its harbor; for on a slumbering ocean, the keel sleeps, too.

Let the winds rush howling forth, and let the waters lift up themselves; though the vessel may rock and her deck may be washed with waves and her mast may creak under the pressure of the full and swelling sail, it is then that she makes headway toward her desired haven. No stars gleam so brightly as those that glisten in the polar sky, no water tastes so sweet as that which springs amid the desert sand, and no faith is so precious as that which lives and triumphs in adversity.

Tried faith brings experience. You could not have believed your own weakness had you not been compelled to pass through the rivers; and you would never have known God's strength had you not been supported amid the water-floods. Faith increases in solidity, assurance, and intensity, the more it is exercised with tribulation. Faith is precious, and its trial is precious, too.

GOD, OUR REFUGE

"The eternal God is your refuge."

DEUTERONOMY 33:27 NKJV

The word "refuge" may be translated "mansion" or "abiding place," which gives the thought that God is our abode, our home. There is a fullness and sweetness in the metaphor, for dear to our hearts is our home, although it be the humblest cottage or the scantiest garret; and dearer far is our blessed God, in whom we live and move and have our being. It is at home that we feel safe: We shut the world out and dwell in quiet security. He is our shelter and retreat, our abiding refuge.

At home we take our rest; it is there we find repose after the fatigue and toil of the day. And so our hearts find rest in God when, wearied with life's conflict, we turn to Him, and our soul dwells at ease. At home, also, we let our hearts loose; we are not afraid of being misunderstood nor of our words being misconstrued. So when we are with God, we can commune freely with Him, laying open all our hidden desires; for if the "secret of the Lord is with them who fear Him," the secrets of them who fear Him ought to be and must be with their Lord.

Home, too, is the place of our truest and purest happiness: and it is in God that our hearts find their deepest delight.

WALK CLOSE TO CHRIST

So walk in Him.

COLOSSIANS 2:6 NKJV

If we have received Christ Himself in our inmost hearts, our new life will manifest its intimate acquaintance with Him by a walk of faith in Him. Walking implies action. Our religion is not to be confined to our closet; we must carry out into practical effect that which we believe. If a man walks in Christ, then he so acts as Christ would act; for Christ being in him his hope, his love, his joy, his life, he is the reflex of the image of Jesus—and men say of that man, "He is like his Master; he lives like Jesus Christ."

Walking signifies progress. Proceed from grace to grace, run forward until you reach the uttermost degree of knowledge that a man can attain concerning our Beloved. Walking implies continuance. There must be a perpetual abiding in Christ. How many Christians think that in the morning and evening they ought to come into the company of Jesus and may then give their hearts to the world all the day. But this is poor living; we should always be with Him, treading in His steps and doing His will.

Walking also implies habit. When we speak of a man's walk and conversation, we mean his habits, the constant tenor of his life. Now if we sometimes enjoy Christ and then forget Him, sometimes call Him ours and again lose our hold, that is not a habit; we do not walk in Him. We must keep to Him, cling to Him, never let Him go but live and have our being in Him.

Not Eternally
Separated by Sin

For as high as the heavens are above the earth, so great is *his* love
for those who fear *him*; as far as the east is from the west,
so far has *he* removed our transgressions from us.
As a father has compassion on his children, so the Lord
has compassion on those who fear *him*.

Psalm 103:11–13 NIV

Does it not make a man glad to know that though once his sins had provoked the Lord they are all blotted out, not one of them remains; though once he was estranged from God and far away from Him by wicked works, yet he is brought near by the blood of Christ. The Lord is no longer an angry judge pursuing us with a drawn sword, but a loving Father into whose bosom we pour our sorrows and find ease for every pang of the heart.

Oh, to know that God actually loves us! I cannot preach upon that theme for it is a subject to muse upon in silence, a matter to sit by the hour together and meditate upon. The Infinite to love an insignificant creature, an ephemera of an hour, a shadow that declines! Is this not a marvel?

For God to pity me, I can understand; for God to condescend to have mercy upon me, I can comprehend; but for Him to love me, for the pure to love a sinner, for the infinitely great to love a reprobate, is matchless, a miracle of miracles! Such thoughts must comfort the soul.

Abba, Father

You did not receive a spirit that makes you a slave again to fear,
but you *received* the Spirit of sonship. And by *him* we *cry*,
"*Abba, Father.*" The Spirit *himself testifies* with our spirit
that we are God's children.

ROMANS 8:15–16 NIV

He cannot be an unhappy man who can cry, "Abba, Father."
The spirit of adoption is always attended by love, joy, and
peace, which are fruits of the Spirit; for we have not received
the spirit of bondage again to fear, but we have received the
spirit of liberty and joy in Christ Jesus. "My God, my Father."
Oh, how sweet the sound.

But all men of God do not enjoy this, you say. Sadly that
is true, but that is their own fault. It is the right and portion
of every believer to live in the assurance that he is reconciled
to God, that God loves him, and that he is God's child, and if
he does not live in that manner, he has himself only to blame.
If there be any starving at God's table, it is because the guest
stints himself, for the feast is superabundant.

If, however, a man comes to live habitually under a sense
of pardon through the sprinkling of the Precious Blood, and
in a delightful sense of perfect reconciliation with the great
God, he is the possessor of a joy unspeakable and full of
glory.

Our Future Is Known by God

Therefore, since we have been justified through faith, we have peace with *God* through our *Lord Jesus Christ*, through whom we have gained access by faith into this grace in which we now stand. And we *rejoice* in the hope of the glory of *God*.

Romans 5:1–2 NIV

The joy of the Lord in the Spirit springs from an assurance that all the future, whatever it may be, is guaranteed by divine goodness; that being children of God, the love of God toward us is not of a mutable character but abides and remains unchangeable. The believer feels an entire satisfaction in leaving himself in the hands of eternal and immutable love.

However happy I may be today, if I am in doubt concerning tomorrow, there is a worm at the root of my peace; although the past may now be sweet in retrospect and the present fair in enjoyment, yet if the future be grim with fear, my joy is but shallow. If my salvation is still a matter of hazard and jeopardy, unmingled joy is not mine and deep peace is still out of my reach.

But when I know that He whom I have rested in has power and grace enough to complete that which He has begun in me and for me, when I see the work of Christ to be no halfway redemption but a complete and eternal salvation, when I perceive that the promises are established upon an unchangeable basis and are in Christ Jesus, ratified by oath and sealed by blood, then my soul has perfect contentment.

THE CROWN OF VICTORY

My sheep *hear my* voice, and *I know* them,
and they *follow me*: And *I give* unto them eternal life;
and they shall never perish, neither shall any man
pluck them out of *my* hand. *My Father*, which gave them *me*,
is greater than all; and no man is able
to pluck them out of *my Father's* hand.

JOHN 10:27–29 KJV

It is true that looking forward there may be seen long avenues of tribulation, but the glory is at the end of them; battles may be foreseen, and woe to the man who does not expect them, but the eye of faith perceives the crown of victory.

Deep waters are mapped upon our journey; but faith can see Jehovah fording these rivers with us, and she anticipates the day when we shall ascend the banks of the shore and enter into Jehovah's rest. When we have received these priceless truths into our souls, we are satisfied with favor and full of the goodness of the Lord.

I value the Gospel not only for what it has done for me in the past, but for the guarantees that it affords me of eternal salvation. "I give unto them eternal life; and they shall never perish, neither shall any man pluck them out of My hand."

GLORY IN TRIBULATIONS

We *glory* in tribulations also.

ROMANS 5:3 KJV

It is joy, when between the millstones crushed like an olive, to yield nothing but the oil of thankfulness; when bruised beneath the flail of tribulation, still to lose nothing but the chaff, and to yield to God the precious grain of entire submissiveness.

Why, this is a little heaven upon earth. To glory in tribulations also, this is a high degree of moving toward the likeness of our Lord. Perhaps the usual communions that we have with our Beloved, though exceedingly precious, will never equal those that we enjoy when we have to break through thorns and briars to be with Him; when we follow Him into the wilderness, then we feel the love of our union to be doubly sweet.

It is a joyous thing when in the midst of mournful circumstances we yet feel that we cannot mourn because the Bridegroom is with us. Blessed is that man who in the most terrible storm is driven—not from his God, but even rides upon the crest of the lofty billows nearer toward heaven. Such happiness is the Christian's lot. I do not say that every Christian possesses it, but I am sure that every Christian ought to do so.

There is a highway to heaven, and all in it are safe; but in the middle of that road there is a special way, an inner path, and all who walk there are happy as well as safe.

Do Not Despair—Pray!

"But we will give ourselves continually to prayer."

ACTS 6:4 NKJV

Great God, help us still to pray, and never from the mercy seat may our footsteps be driven by despair. Our blessed Redeemer persevered in prayer even when the cruel iron tore His tender nerves, and blow after blow of the hammer jarred His whole frame with anguish.

This perseverance may be accounted for by the fact that He was so in the habit of prayer that He could not cease from it. Those long nights upon the cold mountainside, those many days that had been spent in solitude, these had formed in Him a habit so powerful that the severest torments could not stay its force.

Yet it was more than habit. Our Lord was baptized in the spirit of prayer: He lived in it, it lived in Him; it had come to be an element of His nature. He was like that precious spice, which being bruised does not cease to give forth its perfume but rather yields it all the more abundantly because of the blows of the pestle, its fragrance being no outward and superficial quality but an inward virtue essential to its nature, which the pounding in the mortar did not fetch from it, causing it to reveal its secret soul of sweetness.

So Jesus prays, even as a bundle of myrrh gives forth its smell or as birds sing because they cannot do otherwise. Prayer enwrapped His very soul as with a garment, and His heart went forth in such array. Let this be our example—never, under any circumstances, however severe the trial or depressing the difficulty, let us cease from prayer.

RESURRECTION POWER

The power of *his* resurrection. . .

The doctrine of a risen Savior is exceedingly precious. The resurrection is the cornerstone of the entire building of Christianity. It is the keystone of the arch of our salvation. The doctrine is the basis of the experience, but as the flower is lovelier than the root, so is the experience of fellowship with the risen Savior lovelier than the doctrine itself.

I would have you believe that Christ rose from the dead so as to sing of it and derive all the consolation that is possible for you to extract from this well-ascertained and well-witnessed fact; but I beseech you, rest not contented even there. Though you cannot, like the disciples, see Him visibly, yet I bid you aspire to see Christ Jesus by the eye of faith; and though, like Mary Magdalene, you may not "touch" Him, yet may you be privileged to converse with Him and to know that He is risen, you yourselves being risen in Him to newness of life.

To know a crucified Savior as having crucified all my sins is a high degree of knowledge; but to know a risen Savior as having justified me and to realize that He has bestowed upon me new life, having given me to be a new creature through His own newness of life, this is a noble style of experience: Short of it, none ought to rest satisfied. May you both "know Him and the power of His resurrection."

Why should souls who are quickened with Jesus wear the grave clothes of worldliness and unbelief? Rise, for the Lord is risen.

GAZING UPON JESUS

Behold the man!

JOHN 19:5 KJV

If there be one place where our Lord Jesus most fully becomes the joy and comfort of His people, it is where He plunged deepest into the depths of woe. Come, behold the man in the garden of Gethsemane; behold His heart so brimming with love that He cannot hold it in. Behold the bloody sweat as it distills from every pore of His body and falls upon the ground. Behold the man as they drive the nails into His hands and feet. Look up and see the sorrowful image of your suffering Lord. Mark Him as the ruby drops stand on the thorn crown. Behold the man when all His bones are out of joint, and He is poured out like water and brought into the dust of death.

God has forsaken Him, and hell encompasses Him. Behold and see, was there ever sorrow like the sorrow done unto Him?

Gaze upon Him, for if there is no consolation in a crucified Christ, there is no joy in earth or heaven. If in the ransom price of His blood there is not hope, the right hand of God shall know no pleasures forevermore. We have only to sit longer at the cross to be less troubled with our doubts and woes. We have but to see His sorrows, and our sorrows we shall be ashamed to mention. We have but to gaze into His wounds and heal our own.

If we would live correctly, it must be by the contemplation of His death; if we would rise to dignity, it must be by considering His humiliation and His sorrow.

God's Will

Therefore submit to *God.*

JAMES 4:7 NKJV

A throne should be approached with complete submission. We do not pray to God to instruct Him as to what He ought to do, neither for a moment must we presume to dictate the line of the divine procedure. We are permitted to say unto God, "Thus and thus would we have it," but we must furthermore add, "But seeing that we are ignorant and may be mistaken— seeing that we are still in the flesh and therefore may be actuated by carnal motives—not as we will, but as You will."

Who shall dictate to the throne? No loyal child of God will for a moment imagine that he is to occupy the place of the King, but he bows before Him who has a right to be Lord of all; and though he utters his desire earnestly, vehemently, importunately, and pleads and pleads again, yet it is evermore with this needful reservation: "Your will be done, my Lord, and if I ask anything that is not in accordance with it, my inmost will is that You would be good enough to deny Your servant. I will take it as a true answer if You refuse me, if I ask that which seems not good in Your sight."

If we constantly remembered this, we should be less inclined to push certain suits before the throne, for we should feel "I am here in seeking my own ease, my own comfort, my own advantage, and perhaps I may be asking for that which would dishonor God; therefore will I speak with the deepest submission to the divine decrees."

THE THRONE OF GRACE

"Hear from heaven their prayer and their plea,
and *uphold* their cause."

1 KINGS 8:45 NIV

If in prayer I come before a throne of grace, then the faults of my prayer will be overlooked. The groanings of your spirit are such that you think there is nothing in them. What a blotted, blurred, smeared prayer it is. Never mind; you are not come to the throne of justice, otherwise when God perceived the fault in the prayer, He would spurn it—your gaspings and stammerings are before a throne of grace.

When any one of us has presented his best prayer before God, if he saw it as God sees it, he would lament over it; for there is enough sin in the best prayer that was ever prayed to secure its being cast away from God. But our King does not maintain a stately etiquette in His court like that which has been observed by princes, where a little mistake or a flaw would secure the petitioner's being dismissed with disgrace.

No, the faulty cries of His children are not criticized. Our Lord Jesus Christ takes care to alter and amend every prayer before He presents it, and He makes the prayer perfect and prevalent with His own merits. God looks upon the prayer, as presented through Christ, and forgives all its own inherent faultiness. How this ought to encourage any of us who feel ourselves to be feeble, wandering, and unskillful in prayer.

If you feel as if somehow or other you have grown rusty in the act of supplication, never give up, but come still, come more often, for it is a throne of grace to which you come.

Unworthy Man Made Worthy

To *him* who is able to. . .*present* you before
his glorious presence without fault.

Jude 1:24 NIV

Inasmuch as it is a throne of grace, the faults of the petitioner himself shall not prevent the success of his prayer. Oh, what faults there are in us! To come before a throne, how unfit we are—we who are all defiled with sin within and without! Dare any of you think of praying were it not that God's throne is a throne of grace?

An absolute God, infinitely holy and just, could not in consistency with His divine nature answer any prayer from such a sinner as I am, were it not that He has arranged a plan by which my prayer comes up no longer to a throne of absolute justice but to a throne that is also the mercy seat, the propitiation, the place where God meets sinners through Jesus Christ.

I could not say to you, "Pray," not even to you saints, unless it were a throne of grace. A throne of grace is a place fitted for you: Go to your knees; by simple faith go to your Savior, for He, He it is who is the throne of grace. It is in Him that God is able to dispense grace to the most guilty of mankind. Blessed be God; the faults of the prayer shall not shut out our petitions from the God who delights in broken and contrite hearts.

INTERPRETED PLEADINGS

The *Spirit himself intercedes* for us
with groans that words cannot express.

ROMANS 8:26 NIV

If it is a throne of grace, then the desires of the pleader will be interpreted. If I cannot find words in which to utter my desires, God in His grace will read my desires without the words. He takes the meaning of His saints, the meaning of their groans. A throne that was not gracious would not trouble itself to make out our petitions; but God, the infinitely gracious One, will dive into the soul of our desires, and He will read there what we cannot speak with the tongue.

Have you never seen the parent, when his child is trying to say something to him and he knows very well what it is the little one has to say, help him with the words and utter the syllables for him? And so the ever-blessed Spirit, from the throne of grace, will teach us words and write in our hearts the desires themselves.

He will put the desires and the expression of those desires into your spirit by His grace, He will direct your desires to the things that you ought to seek for, He will suggest to you His promises that you may be able to plead them; He will, in fact, be Alpha and Omega to your prayer, just as He is to your salvation, for as salvation is from first to last of grace, so the sinner's approach to the throne of grace is of grace from first to last. What comfort this is. Will we not with the greater boldness draw near to this throne?

GOD KNOWS YOUR PAIN

*You, O Lord, are a God full of compassion,
and gracious, longsuffering and abundant
in mercy and truth.*

PSALM 86:15 NKJV

All the petitioner's miseries shall be compassionated. Suppose I come to the throne of grace with the burden of my sins; there is One on the throne who felt the burden of sin in ages long gone by and has not forgotten its weight. Suppose I come loaded with sorrow; there is One there who knows all the sorrows to which humanity can be subjected. Am I depressed and distressed? Do I fear that God Himself has forsaken me? There is One upon the throne who said, "My God, My God, why have You forsaken Me?"

It is a throne from which grace delights to look upon the miseries of mankind with tender eye, to consider them and to relieve them. Come then you who are not only poor but wretched, whose miseries make you long for death and yet dread it. You captive ones, come in your chains; you slaves, come with the irons upon your souls; you who sit in darkness, come forth all blindfolded as you are.

The throne of grace will look on you, if you cannot look on it, and will give to you, though you have nothing to give in return, and will deliver you, though you cannot raise a finger to deliver yourself.

BE BOLD!

*In him and through faith in him we may
approach God with freedom and confidence.*

EPHESIANS 3:12 NIV

To me it is a most delightful reflection that if I come to the throne of God in prayer, I may feel a thousand defects, but yet there is hope. I usually feel more dissatisfied with my prayers than with anything else I do. We sometimes hear of persons commended for preaching well, but if any shall be enabled to pray well, there will be an equal gift and a higher grace in it.

But suppose in our prayers there should be defects of knowledge: It is a throne of grace, and our Father knows that we have need of these things. Suppose there should be defects of faith: He sees our little faith and still does not reject it, small as it is. He does not in every case measure out His gifts by the degree of our faith, but by the sincerity and trueness of faith.

And if there should be grave defects in our spirit even, and failures in the fervency or in the humility of the prayer, still, though these should not be there and are much to be deplored, grace overlooks all this, forgives all this, and still its merciful hand is stretched out to enrich us according to our needs.

Surely this ought to induce many to pray who have not prayed and should make us who have been long accustomed to use the consecrated art of prayer to draw near with greater boldness than ever to the throne of grace.

THE COVENANT

Ask, and it shall be given you; *seek*, and ye shall find;
knock, and it shall be opened unto you.

MATTHEW 7:7 KJV

On the throne of grace, God is again bound to us by His promises. The covenant contains in it many gracious promises, exceeding great and precious. "Ask, and it shall be given you; seek, and you shall find; knock, and it shall be opened unto you."

Until God had said that word or a word to that effect, it was at His own option to hear prayer or not, but it is not so now; for now if it be true prayer offered through Jesus Christ, His truth binds Him to hear it. A man may be perfectly free, but the moment he makes a promise, he is not free to break it; and the everlasting God wants not to break His promise. He delights to fulfill it.

He has declared that all His promises are "yea and amen" in Christ Jesus; but for our consolation when we survey God under the high and terrible aspect of a sovereign, we have this to reflect on: that He is under covenant bonds of promise to be faithful to the souls who seek Him. His throne must be a throne of grace to His people.

THE BLOOD OF CHRIST

In *Him* we have redemption through *His* blood,
the forgiveness of sins, according to
the riches of *His* grace.

EPHESIANS 1:7 NKJV

Every covenant promise has been endorsed and sealed with blood, and far be it from the everlasting God to pour scorn upon the blood of His dear Son. The signature is the handwriting of God Himself, and the seal is the blood of the Only Begotten. The covenant is ratified with blood, the blood of His own dear Son.

It is not possible that we can plead in vain with God when we plead the blood-sealed covenant, ordered in all things and sure. Heaven and earth shall pass away, but the power of the blood of Jesus with God can never fail. It speaks when we are silent, and it prevails when we are defeated. Better things than that of Abel does it ask for, and its cry is heard.

Let us come boldly, for we hear the promise in our hearts. When we feel alarmed because of the sovereignty of God, let us cheerfully sing—

> "The gospel bears my spirit up,
> A faithful and unchanging God
> Lays the foundation for my hope
> In oaths, and promises, and blood."

IMITATE CHRIST

Be imitators of *God*.

EPHESIANS 5:1 NIV

The Lord Jesus "is altogether lovely." Then if I want to be lovely, I must be like Him, and the model for me as a Christian is Christ. Copy Jesus: "He is altogether lovely." We want to have Christ's zeal, but we must balance it with His prudence and discretion. We must seek to have Christ's love for God, and we must feel His love for men, His forgiveness of injury, His gentleness of speech, His incorruptible truthfulness, His meekness and lowliness, His utter unselfishness, His entire consecration to His Father's business.

Oh, that we had all this! For depend on it—whatever other pattern we select, we have made a mistake; we are not following the true classic model of the Christian artist. Our master model is the "altogether lovely" one. How sweet it is to think of our Lord in the double aspect as our example and our Savior!

The laver that stood in the temple was made of brass: In this the priests washed their feet whenever they offered sacrifices, so does Christ purify us from sin; but the tradition is that this laver was made of very bright brass and acted as a mirror, so that as often as the priests came to it, they could see their own spots in it. Oh, when I come to my Lord Jesus, not only do I get rid of my sins, but also I see my spots in the light of His perfect character; and I am humbled and taught to follow after holiness.

INDISPENSABLE LOVE

Every one that *loveth* is born
of *God*, and *knoweth God*.

1 JOHN 4:7 KJV

There are some graces that in their vigor are not absolutely essential to the bare existence of spiritual life, though very important for its healthy growth; but love for God must be in the heart, or else there is no grace there whatever. If any man does not love God, He is not a renewed man. Love for God is a mark that is always set upon Christ's sheep and never set upon any others. "Every one that loveth is born of God, and knoweth God."

I have no right, therefore, to believe that I am a regenerated person unless my heart truly and sincerely loves God. If I have been regenerated, I may not be perfect, but this one thing I can say, "Lord, You know all things. You know that I love You." When by believing we receive the privilege to become the sons of God, we receive also the nature of sons, and with filial love we cry, "Abba, Father."

There is no exception to this rule: If a man loves not God, neither is he born of God. Show me a fire without heat, then show me regeneration that does not produce love to God; for as the sun must give forth its light, so must a soul that has been created anew by divine grace display its nature by sincere affection toward God. You are not born again unless you love God. How indispensable then is love to God.

LOVE AND OBEY

This is love: that we *walk* in
obedience to *his* commands.

2 JOHN 1:6 NIV

Love is the spring of true obedience. "This is the love of God, that we keep His commandments." Now a man who is not obedient to God's commandments is evidently not a true believer; for although good works do not save us, yet, being saved, believers are sure to produce good works.

Though the fruit is not the root of the tree, yet a well-rooted tree will, in its season, bring forth its fruits. So, though the keeping of the commandments does not make me a child of God, yet, being a child of God, I shall be obedient to my heavenly Father. But this I cannot be unless I love God.

A mere external obedience, a decent formal recognition of the laws of God, is not obedience in God's sight. He abhors the sacrifice where the heart is not found. I must obey because I love, or else I have not in spirit and in truth obeyed at all. See then, that to produce the indispensable fruits of saving faith, there must be love for God; for without it, they would be unreal and indeed impossible.

GOD LOVES YOU

"For God so loved the world that he gave his one and only Son, that whoever believes in him shall not perish but have eternal life."

JOHN 3:16 NIV

It is certain, beloved brethren, that faith in the heart always precedes love. We first believe the love of God for us before we love God in return. And, oh, what an encouraging truth this is. I, a sinner, do not believe that God loves me because I feel I love Him; but I first believe that He loves me, sinner as I am, and then having believed that gracious fact, I come to love my Benefactor in return.

Perhaps some of you seekers are saying to yourselves, "Oh, that we could love God, for then we could hope for mercy." That is not the first step. Your first step is to believe that God loves you, and when that truth is fully fixed in your soul by the Spirit, a fervent love for God will spontaneously issue from your soul, even as flowers willingly pour forth their fragrance under the influence of the dew and the sun.

Every man who ever was saved had to come to God not as a lover of God but as a sinner, and to believe in God's love for him as a sinner.

THE GREATNESS OF GOD'S LOVE

But *God*, being rich in mercy, because of
His great love with which *He loved* us. . .
made us alive together with *Christ*.

EPHESIANS 2:4–5 NASB

Brethren, rest assured that in proportion as we are fully persuaded of God's love for us, we shall be affected with love for Him. Do not let the devil tempt you to believe that God does not love you because your love is feeble; for if he can in any way weaken your belief in God's love for you, he cuts off or diminishes the flow of the streams that feed the sacred grace of love for God.

If I lament that I do not love God as I ought, that is a holy regret; but if I therefore conclude that God's love for me is less because of this, I deny the light because my eye is dim, and I deprive myself also of the power to increase in love.

Let me rather think more and more of the greatness of God's love for me, as I see more and more my unworthiness of it; the more a sinner I am, let me the more fully see how great must be that love that embraces such a sinner as I am; and then as I receive a deeper sense of the divine mercy, I shall feel the more bound to gratitude and constrained to affection. Oh, for a great wave of love to carry us right out into the ocean of love.

COME TO JESUS

Behold, we *come* unto *thee;*
for *thou* art the *Lord* our *God.*

JEREMIAH 3:22 KJV

Does He not declare that He is God and changes not, and therefore you are not consumed? Rekindled are the flames of love in the backslider's bosom when he feels all this to be true; he cries, "Behold, we come unto You for You are the Lord our God." Come just as you are, bad as you are, hardened, cold, dead as you feel yourselves to be; come even so, and believe in the boundless love of God in Christ Jesus.

Then shall come the deep repentance; then shall come the brokenness of heart; then shall come the holy jealousy, the sacred hatred of sin, and the refining of the soul from all her dross; then, indeed, all good things shall come to restore your soul and lead you in the paths of righteousness.

Do not look for these first; that would be looking for the effects before the cause. The great cause of love in the restored backslider must be the love of God for him, to whom he clings with a faith that dares not let go its hold.

ALIKE, YET DIFFERENT

The birds *make* their nests: as for the stork,
the fir trees are her house. The high hills are a refuge
for the wild goats; and the rocks for the conies.

PSALM 104:17–18 KJV

God has not made two creatures precisely alike. You shall gather leaves from a tree, and you shall not find two veined in precisely the same way. In Christian experience it is the same. Wherever there is living Christian experience, it is different from everybody else's experience in some respect. In a family, each child may be like his father, and yet each child shall be different from each other child; and among the children of God, though they all have the likeness of Christ in a measure, yet they are not all exactly like the other.

Are you emptied of self, and do you look to Christ alone? If no other soul has trod the same path as you have, you are on a right path; and though your experience may have eccentricities in it that differ from all others, it is right it should be so. God has not made the wild goat like the coney, nor has He made the stork like any other bird, but He has made each to fit the place it is to occupy; and He makes your experience to be suitable to bring out some point of His glory, which could not be brought out otherwise.

Some are full of rejoicing, others are often depressed, a few keep the happy medium, many soar aloft and then dive into the deeps again; let these varied experiences, as they are all equally clear phases of the same divine loving-kindness, be accepted, and let them be rejoiced in.

A REFUGE FROM FEAR

For *God* has not given us a spirit of fear,
but of power and of love and of a sound mind.

2 TIMOTHY 1:7 NKJV

Beloved, there is a shelter for man from the sense of past guilt. It is because we are guilty that we are fearful: We have broken our Maker's law, and therefore we are afraid. But our Maker came from heaven to earth; Jesus, the Christ of God, came here and was made man and bore our sins that we might never bear His Father's righteous wrath, and whoever believes in Jesus shall find perfect rest in those dear wounds of His.

Since Christ suffered for me, my guilt is gone, my punishment was endured by my Substitute; therefore I hear the voice that says, "Comfort ye, comfort you my people! Say unto them that their warfare is accomplished, for they have received at the Lord's hand double for all their sins."

And as for future fears, He who believes in Jesus finds a refuge from them in the Fatherhood of God. He who trusts Christ says: "Now I have no fear about the present nor about the future. Let catastrophe follow catastrophe, let the world crash and all the universe go to ruin; beneath the wings of the Eternal God, I must be safe. All things must work together for my good, for I love God and have been called according to His purpose." What a blessed shelter this is!

GENUINE WORSHIP

Ascribe to the *LORD* the glory due *his* name.
Bring an offering and *come* before *him*;
worship the *LORD* in the splendor of *his* holiness.

1 CHRONICLES 16:29 NIV

The happiest moments I have ever spent have been occupied with the worship of God. I have never been so near heaven as when adoring before the eternal throne. I think every Christian will bear like witness.

Among all the joys of earth, and I shall not depreciate them, there is no joy comparable to that of praise. The innocent mirth of the fireside, the chaste delights of household love, even these are not to be mentioned side by side with the joy of worship, the rapture of drawing near to the Most High. The purest and most exhilarating joy is the delight of glorifying God, and so anticipating the time when we shall enjoy Him forever. If God's praise has been no wilderness to you, return to it with zest and ardor, and say: "I will yet praise You more and more."

If any suppose that you grow weary with the service of the Lord, tell them that His praise is such freedom, such recreation, such felicity that you desire never to cease from it. As for me, if men call God's service slavery, I desire to be such a bondslave forever and gladly be branded with my Master's name indelibly.

INCREASE YOUR PRAISE

Great is the Lord,
and greatly to be praised.

1 CHRONICLES 16:25 KJV

Every Christian as he grows in grace should have a loftier idea of God. Our highest conception of God falls infinitely short of His glory, but an advanced Christian enjoys a far clearer view of what God is than he had at the first.

Now the greatness of God is ever a claim for praise. "Great is the Lord, and"—what follows?—"greatly to be praised." If then God is greater to me than He was, let my praise be greater.

If I think of Him now more tenderly as my Father—if I have a clearer view of Him in the terror of His justice—if I have a clearer view of the splendors of His wisdom by which He devised the atonement—if I have larger thoughts of His eternal, immutable love—let every advance in knowledge constrain me to say: " 'I will yet praise You more and more.'

"I heard of You by the hearing of the ear, but now my eyes see You: Therefore while I abhor myself in dust and ashes, my praise shall rise yet more loftily; up to Your throne shall my song ascend."

PRAISING MORE OR PRAISING LESS?

Let everything that has
breath *praise* the LORD.

PSALM 150:6 NIV

Are you praising God more and more? If you are not, I am afraid of one thing, and that is that you are probably praising Him less and less. It is a certain truth that if we do not go forward in the Christian life, we go backward. You cannot stand still; there is a drift one way or the other.

Now he who praises God less than he did, and goes on to praise Him less tomorrow and less the next day, and so on—what will he get to? And what is he? Evidently he is one of those who draw back unto perdition, and there are no persons upon whom a more dreadful sentence is pronounced.

May you grow in grace, for life is proven by growth. May you march like pilgrims toward heaven, singing all the way. The lark may serve us as a final picture and an example of what we all should be. We should be mounting: Our prayer should be "Nearer, my God, to Thee." We should be mounting: Our motto might well be "Higher! Higher! Higher!" As we mount, we should sing, and our song should grow louder, clearer, more full of heaven. Upward, brother, I sing as you soar. Upward, sing until you are dissolved in glory.

THE PRAYER OF JABEZ

Oh that *thou* wouldest bless me indeed!

1 CHRONICLES 4:10 KJV

More honorable than his brothers was the child whom his mother bore with sorrow. As for this Jabez, whose aim was so well pointed, his fame so far sounded, his name so lastingly embalmed—he was a man of prayer. The honor he enjoyed would not have been worth having if it had not been vigorously contested and equitably won. His devotion was the key to his promotion. Those are the best honors that come from God, the award of grace with the acknowledgment of service.

The best honor is that which a man gains in communion with the Most High. Jabez, we are told, was more honorable than his brothers, and his prayer is recorded as if to intimate that he was also more prayerful than his brothers. We are told of what petitions his prayer consisted. All through it was very significant and instructive.

"Oh, that You would bless me indeed!" I commend it as a prayer for yourselves, dear brothers and sisters, one that will be available at all seasons, a prayer to begin Christian life with, a prayer to end it with, a prayer that would never be unseasonable in your joys or in your sorrows.

BLESSING AFTER TEARS

Those who *sow* in tears shall *reap* in joy.
He who continually goes forth weeping. . .
shall doubtless come again with rejoicing.

PSALM 126:5-6 NKJV

To a great extent we find that we must sow in tears before we can reap in joy. Many of our works for Christ have cost us tears. Difficulties and disappointments have wrung our soul with anguish. Yet those projects that have cost us more than ordinary sorrow have often turned out to be the most honorable of our undertakings. You may expect a blessing in serving God if you are enabled to persevere under many discouragements.

There are many bounties given to us mercifully by God for which we are bound to be very grateful; but we must not set too much store by them. We may accept them with gratitude, but we must not make them our idols. When we have them, we have great need to cry, "Oh, that You would bless me indeed, and make these inferior blessings real blessings"; and if we have them not, we should with greater vehemence cry, "Oh, that we may be rich in faith, and if not blessed with these external favors, may we be blessed spiritually, and then we shall be blessed indeed."

THE GIFT OF REST

4-13-14 Shawn "Sabbatical"

"Come to Me, all who are weary and heavy-laden, and I will give you rest."

MATTHEW 11:28 NASB

"I will give you rest." "I will give." It is a rest that is a gift, not a rest found in our experience by degrees, but given at once. We come to Jesus; we put out the empty hand of faith, and rest is given us at once most freely. We possess it at once, and it is ours forever. It is a present rest, rest now—not rest after death, not rest after a time of probation and growth and advancement—but it is rest given when we come to Jesus, given there and then.

And it is perfect rest, too, for it is not said nor is it implied that the rest is incomplete. We do not read, "I will give you partial rest," but "rest," as if there were no other form of it. It is perfect and complete in itself. In the blood and righteousness of Jesus, our peace is perfect.

Have you come to Jesus, and has He given you perfect and present rest? If so, I know your eye will catch joyously those two little words, "And I"; and I would implore you lovingly remember the Promiser who speaks. Jesus promises and Jesus performs.

A Petition to God
for His Closeness

Forsake me not, O Lord.

PSALM 38:21 KJV

Frequently we pray that God would not forsake us in the hour of trial and temptation, but we often forget that we have need to use this prayer at all times. There is no moment of our life, however holy, in which we can do without His constant upholding. Whether in light or in darkness, in communion or in temptation, we alike need the prayer "Forsake me not, O Lord."

We cannot do without continued aid from above; let it then be your prayer today, "Forsake me not. Father, forsake not Your child, lest he fall by the hand of the enemy. Shepherd, forsake not Your lamb, lest he wander from the safety of the fold. Great Husbandman, forsake not Your plant, lest it wither and die. 'Forsake me not, O Lord,' now—and forsake me not at any moment of my life.

Forsake me not in my joys, lest they absorb my heart. Forsake me not in my sorrows, lest I murmur against You. Forsake me not in the day of my repentance, lest I lose the hope of pardon and fall into despair; and forsake me not in the day of my strongest faith, lest faith degenerate into presumption. Forsake me not, for without You I am weak, but with You I am strong. Forsake me not, for my path is dangerous and full of snares, and I cannot do without Your guidance. 'Be not far from me, O Lord, for trouble is near, for there is none to help. Leave me not, neither forsake me, O God of my salvation!' "

JOY IN PERSECUTION

If any man will come after me, *let him* deny *himself,*
and take *up his cross daily, and* follow me.

LUKE 9:23 KJV

You must be willing to bear Christ's burden. Now the burden of Christ is His cross, which every Christian must take up. Expect to be reproached, expect to meet with some degree of the scandal of the cross, for the offense of it never ceases. Persecution and reproach are a blessed burden; when your soul loves Jesus, it is a joyful thing to suffer for Him, and therefore never, by any cowardly retirement or refusal to profess your faith, evade your share of this honorable load.

Woe unto those who say, "I will never be a martyr." No rest is sweeter than the martyr's rest. Woe unto those who say, "We will go to heaven by night along a secret road and so avoid the shame of the cross." The rest of the Christian is found not in cowardice but in courage; it lies not in providing for ease but in the brave endurance of suffering for the truth.

The restful spirit counts the reproach of Christ to be greater riches than all treasures; he falls in love with the cross and counts the burden light, and so finds rest in service and rest in suffering.

Rest for God's People

There remaineth therefore a rest to the people of *God*.
For he that is entered into his rest, he also hath
ceased from his own works, as *God* did from *his*.
Let us *labour* therefore to enter into that rest.

Hebrews 4:9–11 KJV

It is very evident that the rest that we are to find is a rest that grows entirely out of our spirits being conformed to the spirit of Christ. "Learn of Me, and you shall find rest." It is then a spiritual rest altogether independent of circumstances.

It is a vain idea of ours to suppose that if our circumstances were altered we should be more at rest. My brother, if you cannot rest in poverty, neither would you in riches; if you cannot rest in the midst of persecution, neither would you in the midst of honor. It is the spirit within that gives the rest; that rest has little to do with anything without.

The spirit is the spring of rest; as for the outward surroundings, they are of small account. Let your mind be like the mind of Christ, and you shall find rest unto your souls: a deep rest, a growing rest, a rest found out more and more, an abiding rest, not only that you have found, but that you shall go on to find.

Pray, Rejoice, Give Thanks

Rejoice evermore. *Pray* without ceasing.
In every thing *give* thanks.

1 Thessalonians 5:16–18 KJV

"Pray without ceasing." Observe what it follows. It comes immediately after the precept "Rejoice evermore," as if that command had somewhat staggered the reader and made him ask, "How can I always rejoice?" and therefore the apostle appended as answer, "Always pray." The more praying, the more rejoicing.

Prayer gives a channel to the pent-up sorrows of the soul; they flow away, and in their stead streams of sacred delight pour into the heart. At the same time the more rejoicing, the more praying; when the heart is in a quiet condition and full of joy in the Lord, then also will it be sure to draw near to the Lord in worship. Holy joy and prayer act and react upon each other.

Observe, however, what immediately follows the text: "In every thing give thanks." When joy and prayer are married, their firstborn child is gratitude. When we joy in God for what we have and believingly pray to Him for more, then our souls thank Him both in the enjoyment of what we have and in the prospect of what is yet to come.

Those three texts are three companion pictures, representing the life of a true Christian. These three precepts are an ornament of grace to every believer's neck; wear them, every one of you, for glory and for beauty: "Rejoice evermore"; "Pray without ceasing"; "In every thing give thanks."

PRAY AT ANY TIME

Evening, and morning, and at noon, will I pray,
and cry aloud: and *he* shall hear my voice.

PSALM 55:17 KJV

"Pray without ceasing." Our Lord Jesus Christ in these words assures you that you may pray without ceasing. There is no time when we may not pray. You have permission given to come to the mercy seat when you will, for the veil of the most holy place is torn from the top to the bottom, and our access to the mercy seat is undisputed and indisputable.

Kings hold their receptions upon certain appointed days, and then their courtiers are admitted; but the King of kings holds a constant reception. The dead of night is not too late for God; the breaking of the morning, when the first gray light is seen, is not too early for the Most High; at midday He is not too busy; and when the evening gathers, He is not weary with His children's prayers. "Pray without ceasing" is a most sweet and precious permit to the believer to pour out his heart at all times before the Lord.

The doors of the temple of divine love shall not be shut. Nothing can set a barrier between a praying soul and its God. The road of angels and of prayers is ever open. Let us but send out the dove of prayer, and we may be certain that she will return to us with an olive branch of peace in her mouth. The Lord continually regards the pleadings of His servants and waits to be gracious to them.

PERSECUTION WILL
LEAD TO GLORY

Everyone who wants to live a godly
life in *Christ Jesus* will be persecuted.

2 TIMOTHY 3:12 NIV

It is by no means pleasant to be opposed in doing right by those who ought to help us in it. It is very painful to flesh and blood to go contrary to those we love. What is more, those who hate Christians have a way of reviling so that they are sure to make us wince. They watch our weak points, and with very wonderful skill, they turn their discoveries to account. If one thing is more provoking than another, they will be sure to say it, and say it when we are least able to bear it.

It may be they are very polite people, and if so, your refined persecutors have a very dainty way of cutting to the bone and yet smiling all the while. They can say a malicious thing so delicately that you can neither resent it nor endure it. They are perfect masters of it and know how to make the iron enter into the soul.

Do not be astonished, therefore, if you are sorely vexed, neither be amazed as though some strange thing happened to you. The martyrs did not suffer sham pains; the racks on which they were stretched were not beds of ease, nor were their prisons rooms of comfort. Their pains were agonies; their martyrdoms were torments.

If you had sham griefs, you might expect counterfeit joys; let the reality of your tribulation assure you of the reality of the coming glory.

CHEERFUL THROUGH PERSECUTION

We are. . .persecuted, but not forsaken.

2 CORINTHIANS 4:8-9 KJV

Persecution will try your love to Jesus. If you really love Him, you will cheerfully stand in the humiliation of reproach with Him, and when enemies have rubbish to hurl, you will say, "Throw it upon me rather than upon Him; if there is a harsh thing to be said, say it about me rather than against my Lord."

It will try your love, I say, and so it will all your graces in their turn; and this is good for you. These virtues will not increase in strength unless they are brought into action, and if they are not tested, who is to know of what sort they are? Your valiant soldier in quiet barracks at home could fight, no doubt, but how do you know until he has passed through a battle? He who has charged up to the cannon's mouth, he who is adorned with a saber cut across his brow and bears many wounds beside which he gained in the service of his king, he is brave beyond question.

Good gold must expect to be tried in the fire, and these oppositions are sent on purpose that our faith and our love and all our graces should be proved genuine by enduring the test.

THE OIL OF GLADNESS

You love righteousness and *hate* wickedness; Therefore *God,*
Your God, has anointed *You* with the oil of gladness
more than *Your* companions.

PSALM 45:7 NKJV

You cannot conceive the gladness of Christ. If you have ever
brought one soul to Christ, you have had a drop of it; but His
gladness lies not only in receiving them, but also in actually
being the author of salvation to every one of them.

The Savior looks upon the redeemed with an unspeakable delight, thinks of what they used to be, thinks of what
they would have been but for His interposition, thinks of
what they now are, thinks of what He means to make them in
that great day when they shall rise from the dead; and as His
heart is full of love for them, He joys in their joy and exults
in their exultation.

I speak with humblest fear lest in any word I should speak
amiss, for He is God as well as man; but this is certain, that
there is a joy of our Lord into which He will give His faithful
ones to enter, a joy that He has won by passing through the
shame and grief by which He has redeemed mankind. The oil
of gladness is abundantly poured on that head that once was
crowned with thorns.

GOD'S WILL UPHOLDS US THROUGH TRIALS

I am crucified with Christ: nevertheless I live;
yet not I, but Christ liveth in me.

GALATIANS 2:20 KJV

We should receive chastisement with meek submission, presenting ourselves to God that He may do with us still as He has dealt with us—not wishing to move to the right hand or to the left: asking Him if it may be His will to remove the load, to heal the pain, to deliver us from the bereavement, and the like, but still always leaving ample margin for full resignation of spirit.

The gold is not to rebel against the goldsmith, but should at once yield to be placed in the crucible and thrust into the fire. The wheat as it lies upon the threshing floor is not to have a will of its own, but to be willing to endure the strokes of the flail that the chaff may be separated from the precious corn. We are not far off being purged from dross and cleansed from chaff when we are perfectly willing to undergo any process that the divine wisdom may appoint us.

Self and sin are married and will never be divorced, and until our selfhood is crushed, the seed of sin will still have abundant vitality in it; but when it is "not I" but "Christ who liveth in me," then have we come near to that mark to which God has called us and to which, by His Spirit, He is leading us.

The Will of God

"Then they will seek My face;
in their affliction they will earnestly seek Me."

HOSEA 5:15 NKJV

We should accept chastisement cheerfully. It is a hard lesson, but a lesson that the Comforter is able to teach us—to be glad that God should have His way. Do you know what it is sometimes to be very pleased to do what you do not like to do? I mean you would not have liked to do it, but you find that it pleases someone you love, and straightaway the irksome task becomes a pleasure.

Have you not felt sometimes, when one whom you very much esteem is sick and ill, that you would be glad enough to bear the pain, at least for a day or two, that you might give the suffering one a little rest? Would you not find a pleasure in being an invalid for a while to let your beloved one enjoy a season of health?

Let the same motive, in a higher degree, sway your spirit! Try to feel, "If it pleases God, it pleases me. If, Lord, it is Your will, it shall be my will. Let the lashes of the scourge be multiplied, if then You will be the more honored and I shall be permitted to bring You some degree of glory." The cross becomes sweet when our health is so sweetened by the Spirit that our will runs parallel with the will of God.

We should learn to say, in the language of Elihu, "I have borne, I do bear, I accept it all."

FORGIVENESS OF SINS

"Everyone who *believes* in *him receives*
forgiveness of sins through *his* name."

ACTS 10:43 NIV

All our transgressions are swept away at once, carried off as by a flood, and so completely removed from us that no guilty trace of them remains. They are all gone! Oh, believers, think of this, for it is no little thing. Sins against a holy God, sins against His loving Son, sins against the Gospel as well as against the law, sins against man as well as against God, sins of the body as well as sins of the mind, sins as numerous as the sands on the seashore and as great as the sea itself: All, all are removed from us as far as the east is from the west.

All this evil was rolled into one great mass and laid upon Jesus, and having borne it all, He has made an end of it forever. When the Lord forgave us, He forgave us the whole debt. He did not take the bill and say, "I strike out this item and that," but the pen went through it all: Paid. It was a receipt in full of all demands; Jesus took the handwriting that was against us and nailed it to His cross, to show before the entire universe that its power to condemn us had ceased forever.

We have in Him a full forgiveness.

Our Sins Are Forgotten

Their sins and iniquities will
I remember no more.

Hebrews 10:17 KJV

There is such a truth, reality, and emphasis in the pardon of God as you can never find in the pardon of man; for though a man should forgive all you have done against him, if you have treated him very badly, yet it is more than you could expect that he should also forget it, but the Lord says, "Their sins and iniquities will I remember no more forever."

If a man has sinned against you, although you have forgiven him, you are not likely to trust him again. But see how the Lord deals with His people. The Lord lets bygones be bygones so completely that He trusts pardoned souls with His secrets, for "the secret of the Lord is with them who fear Him"; and He entrusts some of us with His choicest treasures.

Let us rejoice in that grand promise that comes to us by the mouth of Jeremiah of old, "In those days, and in that time, saith the Lord, the iniquity of Israel shall be sought for, and there shall be none; and the sins of Judah, and they shall not be found: for I will pardon them whom I reserve."

Here is annihilation—the only annihilation I know of—the absolute annihilation of sin through the pardon that the Lord gives to His people. Let us sing it as though it were a choice hymn: "The iniquity of Israel shall be sought for, and there shall be none."

Forgiving Others

Be kind. . .forgiving one another,
even as *God* in *Christ forgave* you.

EPHESIANS 4:32 NKJV

Observe how the apostle puts it. Does he say, "forgiving another"? No, that is not the text, if you look at it. It is "forgiving
one another." One another! Ah, then that means that if you
have to forgive today, it is very likely that you will yourself
need to be forgiven tomorrow, for it is "forgiving one another."
It is a mutual operation, a cooperative service. You forgive me,
and I forgive you, and we forgive them, and they forgive us,
and so a circle of unlimited forbearance and love goes around
the world.

There is something wrong about me that needs to be forgiven by my brother, but there is also something wrong about
my brother that needs to be forgiven by me, and this is what
the apostle means—that we are all mutually to be exercising
the sacred art and mystery of forgiving one another. If we
always did this, we should not endure those who have a special faculty for spying out faults.

You may know very well what a man is by what he says of
others. It is a gauge of character that very seldom will deceive
you, to judge other men by their own judgment of their fel-
lows. Their speech betrays their heart. Show me your tongue.
He who speaks with an ill tongue about his neighbor has an ill
heart; rest assured of that.

We shall have a great deal to forgive in other people, but
there will be a great deal more to be forgiven in ourselves.

VENGEANCE IS
RESERVED FOR GOD

Vengeance is *mine*;
I will repay, saith the *Lord*.

ROMANS 12:19 KJV

Never in any way, directly or indirectly, avenge yourselves. For any fault that is ever done to you, the Master says to you, "Resist not evil." In all things bend, bow, yield, submit.

Brother, the most splendid vengeance you can ever have is to do good to those who do evil to you and to speak well of those who speak ill of you. They will be ashamed to look at you; they will never hurt you again if they see that you cannot be provoked except it be to greater love and larger kindness. This ought to be the mark of Christians; not "I will have the law reprimand you" or "I will avenge myself," but "I will bear and forbear even to the end."

"Vengeance is Mine. I will repay, saith the Lord." Do not take that into your hand that God says belongs to Him, but as He for Christ's sake has forgiven you, so also forgive all those who do you wrong.

"How long am I to do that?" one asks. "I would not mind doing it three or four times." There was one of old who would go the length of six or seven, but Jesus Christ said "unto seventy times seven." That is a very considerable number. You may count whether you have yet reached that amount, and if you have, you will now be glad to begin again, still forgiving, even as God for Christ's sake has forgiven you.

MEDITATION ON SCRIPTURE

*"Have you not read? If you had
known what this means. . ."*

MATTHEW 12:3, 7 NKJV

If you are to understand what you read, you will need to meditate upon it. Some passages of scripture lie clear before us—blessed shallows in which the lambs may wade—but there are deeps in which our mind might rather drown itself than swim with pleasure, if it came there without caution.

There are texts of scripture that are made and constructed on purpose to make us think. Many of the veils that are cast over scripture are not meant to hide the meaning from the diligent but to compel the mind to be active, for often the diligence of the heart in seeking to know the divine mind does the heart more good than the knowledge itself.

Meditation and careful thought exercise us and strengthen us for the reception of the yet more lofty truths. We must meditate. The Word of God is always most precious to the man who most lives upon it.

With God's Word it is well for us to be like squirrels, living in it and living on it. Let us exercise our minds by leaping from bough to bough of it, find our rest and food in it, and make it our all in all. We shall be the people who get the profit out of it if we make it to be our food, our medicine, our treasury, our armory, our rest, our delight. May the Holy Spirit lead us to do this and make the Word so precious to our souls.

Prayer to Understand the Bible

The meditation of my heart
shall be of understanding.

Psalm 49:3 KJV

It is a grand thing to be driven to think; it is a grander thing to be driven to pray through having been made to think. Am I not addressing some of you who do not read the Word of God, and am I not speaking to many more who do read it but do not read it with the strong resolve that they will understand it? I know it must be so. Do you wish to begin to be true readers? Will you from this time forth labor to understand?

Then you must get to your knees. You must cry to God for direction. Who understands a book best? The author of it. So, beloved, the Holy Spirit is with us, and when we take His book and begin to read and want to know what it means, we must ask the Holy Spirit to reveal the meaning. He will not work a miracle, but He will elevate our minds; and He will suggest to us thoughts that will lead us on by their natural relation, the one to the other, until at last we come to the core of His divine instruction.

Seek then very earnestly the guidance of the Holy Spirit, for if the very soul of reading be the understanding of what we read, then we must in prayer call upon the Holy Spirit to unlock the secret mysteries of the inspired Word.

A CRY FOR MERCY

God be merciful to me a sinner.

LUKE 18:13 KJV

Let us praise His name because you and I are still spared to pray and permitted to pray. What if we are greatly afflicted, yet it is of the Lord's mercy that we are not consumed. If we had received our deserts, we should not now have been on praying ground and pleading terms with Him. But let it be for our comfort and to God's praise that still we may stand with bowed head and cry each one, "God, be merciful to me, a sinner."

Still may we cry like sinking Peter, "Lord, save me, or I perish." Like David, we may be unable to go up to the temple, but we can still go to our God in prayer. Therefore let us give thanks to God that He has nowhere said to us, "Seek My face in vain."

If we find a desire to pray trembling within our soul, and if though almost extinct we feel some hope in the promise of our gracious God, if our heart still groans after holiness and after God, though she has lost her power to pray with joyful confidence as once she did, yet let us be thankful that we can pray even if it be but a little.

In the will and power to pray, there lies the capacity for infinite blessedness: He who has the key of prayer can open heaven; yes, he has access to the heart of God. Therefore bless God for prayer.

THANKSGIVING AND REQUESTS

Let your requests be made known to God.

PHILIPPIANS 4:6 NKJV

Beloved, beyond the fact of prayer and our power to exercise it, there is a further ground of thanksgiving that we have already received great mercy at God's hands. We are not coming to God to ask favors and receive them for the first time in our lives. Why, blessed be His name if He never granted me another favor; I have enough for which to thank Him as long as I have any being.

And this, furthermore, is to be recollected: That whatever great things we are about to ask, we cannot possibly be seeking for blessings one-half so great as those that we have already received if we are indeed His children. If you are a Christian, you have life in Christ. Are you about to ask for food and clothing? Life is more than these. You have already obtained Christ Jesus to be yours, and He who spared Him not will not deny you anything.

Let us perpetually thank our Benefactor for what we have while we make requests for something more. Shall not the abundant utterances of the memory of His great goodness run over into our requests, until our petitions are baptized in gratitude. While we come before God in one aspect empty-handed to receive of His goodness, on the other hand we should never appear before Him empty, but come with the fat of our sacrifices, offering praise and glorifying God.

A THANKFUL SPIRIT

Through *Him* then, *let* us continually
offer up a sacrifice of praise to *God*, that is,
the fruit of lips that give thanks to *His* name.

HEBREWS 13:15 NASB

I believe that when a man begins to pray with thanksgiving, he is upon the eve of receiving the blessing. God's time to bless you has come when you begin to praise Him as well as pray to Him. God has His set time to favor us, and He will not grant us our desire until the due season has arrived. But the time has come when you begin to bless the Lord.

Our thanksgiving will show that the reason for our waiting is now exhausted; that the waiting has answered its purpose, and we may now come to a joyful end. Sometimes we are not in a fit state to receive a blessing, but when we reach the condition of thankfulness, then is the time when it is safe for God to indulge us. If you will but desire God to be glorified and aim at glorifying Him yourself, then the joys of true godliness will come to you in answer to prayer.

The time for the blessing is when you begin to praise God for it. For, brethren, you may be sure that when you offer thanksgiving on the ground that God has answered your prayer, you really have prevailed with God.

Work as for the Lord

Therefore, whether you *eat* or *drink*,
or whatever you do, do all to the glory of *God*.

1 Corinthians 10:31 NKJV

Do we perhaps limit our estimate of serving God? You say, "I cannot serve God," when you cannot teach in the school or preach in the pulpit, when you are unable to sit on a committee or speak on a platform, as if these were the only forms of service to be taken into account. Do you not think that a mother nursing her baby is serving God? Do you not think that men and women going about their daily labor with patient diligence, fulfilling the duties of domestic life are serving God? If you think correctly, you will understand that they are.

The servant sweeping the room, the mistress preparing the meal, the workman driving a nail, the merchant completing his ledger ought to do all in the service of God. Though it is very desirable that we should each have some definitely religious work before us, yet it is much better that we should hallow our common skill and make our ordinary work chime with the melodies of a soul attuned for heaven.

Let true religion be our life, and then our life will be true religion. Let the stream of your common life as it flows on be holy and courageous; you will find that you shall not be neglected or overlooked who simply sit at Jesus' feet and listen to His words when you can do no more. This is service done for Him that He can appreciate; complain who may.

FAITH

Take up the shield of faith, with which you can *extinguish*
all the flaming arrows of the evil one.

EPHESIANS 6:16 NIV

Faith is that blessed grace that is most pleasing to God, and thus it is the most displeasing to the devil. By faith God is greatly glorified, and consequently by faith Satan is greatly annoyed. He rages at faith because he sees his own defeat and the victory of grace.

It is by our faith that we are saved, justified, and brought near to God, and therefore it is no marvel that it is attacked. It is by believing in Christ that we are delivered from the reigning power of sin and receive power to become the sons of God. Faith is as vital to salvation as the heart is vital to the body; for this reason the javelins of the enemy are mainly aimed at this essential grace.

Faith is the standard-bearer, and the object of the enemy is to strike him down that the battle may be gained. All the powers of darkness that are opposed to right and truth are sure to fight against our faith, and manifold temptations will march in their legions against our confidence in God.

It is by our faith that we live; we began to live by it and continue to live by it. Faith is your jewel, your joy, your glory; and the thieves who haunt the pilgrim's way are all scheming to tear it from you. Hold fast; this your choice treasure.

GROW IN ALL GRACE

Grow in grace, and in the knowledge
of our *Lord* and *Saviour Jesus Christ.*

2 PETER 3:18 KJV

"Grow in grace"—not in one grace only but in all grace. Grow in the starting place of grace: faith. Believe the promises more firmly than you have before. Let faith increase in fullness, constancy, simplicity. Grow also in love. Ask that your love may become extended, more intense, more practical, influencing every thought, word, and deed. Grow likewise in humility. Seek to lie very low and know more of your own nothingness.

As you grow downward in humility, seek also to grow upward—having nearer approaches to God in prayer and more intimate fellowship with Jesus. To know Him is "life eternal," and to advance in the knowledge of Him is to increase in happiness. Whoever has sipped this wine will thirst for more, for although Christ satisfies, yet it is such a satisfaction, that the appetite is not satisfied but whetted.

If you know the love of Jesus, so will you pant after deeper draughts of His love. If you do not desire to know Him better, then you love Him not, for love always cries, "Nearer, nearer." Seek to know more of Him in His divine nature, in His human relationship,in His finished work, in His death, in His resurrection, in His present glorious intercession, and in His future royal advent. Remain by the cross and search the mystery of His wounds.

An increase of love for Jesus, and a more perfect apprehension of His love for us, is one of the best tests of growth in grace.

CASTING OUR CARES ON JESUS

Casting all your care upon *him*;
for *he careth* for you.

1 PETER 5:7 KJV

It is a happy way of soothing sorrow when we feel "He cares for me." Come, cast your burden upon your Lord. You are staggering beneath a weight that your Father would not feel. What seems to you a crushing burden would be to Him but as dust.

Oh, child of suffering, be patient; God has not passed you over in His providence. He who is the feeder of sparrows will also furnish you with what you need. Do not sit down in despair; hope on, hope ever. There is One who cares for you. His eye is fixed on you, His heart beats with pity for your woe, and His hand omnipotent will bring you the needed help. He, if you are one of His family, will bind up your wounds and heal your broken heart. Do not doubt His grace because of your tribulation, but believe that He loves you as much in seasons of trouble as in times of happiness.

What a serene and quiet life might you lead if you would leave providing to the God of providence! If God cares for you, why should you care, too? Can you trust Him for your soul and not for your body? He has never refused to bear your burdens; He has never fainted under their weight. Come then, soul! Cease fretting, and leave all your concerns in the hand of a gracious God.

CRIES FOR HELP

Beginning to *sink* he cried out,
saying, *"Lord, save me!"*

MATTHEW 14:30 NKJV

Sinking times are praying times with the Lord's servants. Peter neglected prayer at the start of his venturous journey; but when he began to sink, his danger made him a beggar, and his cry, though late, was not too late. In our hours of bodily pain and mental anguish, we find ourselves naturally driven to prayer. The tried believer hastens to the mercy seat for safety; heaven's great harbor of refuge is prayer.

Short prayers are long enough. There were only three words in the petition that Peter grasped, but they were sufficient for his purpose. Not length but strength is desirable. A sense of need is a mighty teacher of brevity. All that is real prayer in many a long address might have been uttered in a petition as short as that of Peter.

Our boundaries are the Lord's opportunities. Immediately a keen sense of danger forces an anxious cry. The ear of Jesus hears, and with Him ear and heart go together and the hand does not long linger. At the last moment, we appeal to our Master, but His swift hand makes up for our delays by instant and effectual action.

Are we nearly engulfed by the boisterous waters of affliction? Let us then lift up our souls unto our Savior, and we may rest assured that He will not suffer us to perish. When we can do nothing, Jesus can do all things; let us enlist His powerful aid upon our side, and all will be well.

GOD'S PROMISES

"Do as You have said."

2 SAMUEL 7:25 NKJV

God's promises were never meant to be thrown aside as waste paper; He intended that they should be used. Nothing pleases our Lord better than to see His promises put in circulation; He loves to see His children bring them up to Him and say, "Lord, do as You have said." We glorify God when we plead His promises.

Faith lays hold upon the promise of pardon, and it does not delay, saying, "This is a precious promise; I wonder if it be true?" but it goes straight to the throne with it and pleads, "Lord, here is the promise—do as You have said."

Our Lord replies, "Let it be done even as you will." When a Christian grasps a promise, if he does not take it to God, he dishonors Him; but when he hastens to the throne of grace and cries, "Lord, I have nothing to recommend me but this: You have said it," then his desire will be granted. Our heavenly Banker delights to cash His own notes. Never let the promise rust. Draw the word of promise out of its cover, and use it with holy violence.

Do not think that God will be troubled by your importunately reminding Him of His promises. He loves to hear the loud outcries of needy souls. It is His delight to bestow favors. He is more ready to hear than you are to ask. It is God's nature to keep His promises; therefore go at once to the throne with "Do as You have said."

OUR CHOSEN CHRIST

I have exalted one chosen out of the people.

PSALM 89:19 KJV

Why was Christ chosen out of the people? Speak, my heart, for heart thoughts are best. Was it not that He might be able to be our brother in the blessed tie of kindred blood? Oh, what relationship there is between Christ and the believer! The believer can say, "I have a Brother in heaven; I may be poor, but I have a Brother who is rich and is a King. He loves me; He is my Brother."

Believer, wear this blessed thought like a necklace of diamonds around the neck of your memory; put it as a golden ring on the finger of recollection, and use it as the King's own seal, stamping the petitions of your faith with confidence of success. He is a brother born for adversity; treat Him as such.

Christ was also chosen out of the people that He might know our wants and sympathize with us. "He was tempted in all points like as we are, yet without sin." In all our sorrows we have His sympathy. Temptation, pain, disappointment, weakness, weariness, poverty—He knows them all, for He has felt all. Remember this, Christian, and let it comfort you.

However difficult and painful your road, it is marked by the footsteps of your Savior; and even when you reach the dark valley of the shadow of death, you will find His footprints there. Wherever we go, He has been our forerunner; each burden we have to carry has once been laid on the shoulders of Immanuel.

DELIVERANCE FROM DANGER

Surely *He* shall *deliver* you
from the snare of the fowler.

PSALM 91:3 NKJV

God delivers His people from the snare of the fowler in two senses. First, He delivers them from the snare—does not let them enter it—and second, if they should be caught in it, He delivers them out of it.

"He shall deliver you from the snare." How? Trouble is often the means whereby God delivers us. God knows that our backsliding will soon end in our destruction, and He in mercy sends the rod. We say, "Lord, why is this?" not knowing that our trouble has been the means of delivering us from far greater evil. Many have been saved from ruin by their sorrows and their crosses.

At other times, God keeps His people from the snare of the fowler by giving them great spiritual strength, so that when they are tempted to do evil, they say, "How can I do this great wickedness and sin against God?"

But what a blessed thing it is that if the believer shall, in an evil hour, fall into the net; God will bring him out of it! Backslider, be cast down, but do not despair. Although you have been wandering, hear what your Redeemer says: "Return, backsliding children; I will have mercy upon you." You shall yet be brought out of all evil into which you have fallen, and though you shall never cease to repent of your ways, yet He who loves you will not cast you away; He will receive you and give you joy and gladness.

STRENGTHEN, O GOD

Strengthen, O *God*, that which
thou hast wrought for us.

PSALM 68:28 KJV

It is our wisdom as well as our necessity to beseech God continually to strengthen "that which He has wrought in us." It is because of their neglect in this that many Christians may blame themselves for those trials and afflictions that arise from unbelief.

We often forget that the Author of our faith must be the Preserver of it, also. The lamp burning in the temple was never allowed to go out, but it had to be daily replenished with fresh oil; in like manner, our faith can only live by being sustained with the oil of grace, and we can only obtain this from God Himself.

He who built the world upholds it, or it would fall in one tremendous crash; He who made us Christians must maintain us by His Spirit, or our ruin will be speedy and final. Let us then go to our Lord for the grace and strength we need. Do you think He will fail to protect and sustain? Only let your faith take hold of His strength, and all the powers of darkness, led on by the master fiend of hell, cannot cast a cloud or shadow over your joy and peace.

Why faint when you may be strong? Why suffer defeat when you may conquer? Take your wavering faith and drooping graces to Him who can revive and replenish them, and earnestly pray, "Strengthen, O God, that which thou hast wrought for us."

THE UNSEEN PRIZE

The things which are not seen. . .

2 CORINTHIANS 4:18 KJV

In our Christian pilgrimage, it is well, for the most part, to be looking forward. Forward lies the crown, and onward is the goal. Whether it be for hope, for joy, for consolation, or for the inspiring of our love, the future must, after all, be the grand object of the eye of faith. Looking into the future, we see sin cast out, the body of sin and death destroyed, the soul made perfect and fit to be a partaker of the inheritance of the saints in light.

Looking further yet, the believer's enlightened eye can see death's river passed, the gloomy stream forded, and the hills of light attained on which stands the celestial city; he sees himself enter within the pearly gates, hailed as more than conqueror, crowned by the hand of Christ, embraced in the arms of Jesus, glorified with Him, and made to sit together with Him on His throne, even as He has overcome and has sat down with the Father on His throne.

The thought of this future may well relieve the darkness of the past and the gloom of the present. The joys of heaven will surely compensate for the sorrows of earth. Hush, my fears! This world is but a narrow span, and you shall soon have passed it. Hush, hush, my doubts! Death is but a narrow stream, and you shall soon have forded it. Time, how short— eternity, how long! Death, how brief—immortality, how endless! The road is so, so short! I shall soon be there.

PERFECT IN JESUS

"The LORD Our Righteousness. . ."

JEREMIAH 23:6 NIV

It will always give a Christian the greatest calm, quiet, ease, and peace to think of the perfect righteousness of Christ. How often are the saints of God downcast and sad! I do not think they would be if they could always see their perfection in Christ. There are some who are always talking about corruption and the depravity of the heart and the innate evil of the soul. This is quite true, but why not go a little further and remember that we are "perfect in Christ Jesus."

It is no wonder that those who are dwelling upon their own corruption should wear such downcast looks; but surely if we call to mind that "Christ is made unto us righteousness," we shall be of good cheer. Though distresses afflict me, though Satan assault me, though there may be many things to be experienced before I get to heaven, those are done for me in the covenant of divine grace; there is nothing wanting in my Lord.

Christ has done it all. On the cross He said, "It is finished!" and if it is finished, then I am complete in Him and can rejoice with joy unspeakable and full of glory. You will not find on this side of heaven a holier people than those who receive into their hearts the doctrine of Christ's righteousness.

A MIRROR IMAGE OF JESUS

They *marveled*. And they *realized*
that they had been with Jesus.

ACTS 4:13 NKJV

A Christian should be a striking likeness of Jesus Christ. If we were what we profess to be and what we should be, we should be pictures of Christ—yes, such striking likenesses of Him that the world would not have to hold us up and say, "He seems somewhat of a likeness"; but they would, when they once beheld us, exclaim, "He has been with Jesus, he has been taught of Him, he is like Him, he has caught the very idea of the holy Man of Nazareth, and he demonstrates it in his life and everyday actions."

A Christian should be like Christ in his boldness. Be like Jesus, valiant for your God. Imitate Him in your loving spirit; think kindly, speak kindly, and do kindly, that men may say of you, "He has been with Jesus." Imitate Jesus in His holiness. Was He zealous for His Master? So should you be; ever go about doing good. Was He self-denying, never looking to His own interest? Be the same. Was He devout? Be fervent in your prayers. Had He deference to His Father's will? So submit yourselves to Him. Was He patient? So learn to endure.

And best of all, as the highest portraiture of Jesus, try to forgive your enemies as He did. Forgive as you hope to be forgiven. Heap coals of fire on the head of your foe by your kindness to him.

In all ways and by all means, so live that all may say of you, "He has been with Jesus."

GROWING IN GRACE

"Show me why You contend with me."

JOB 40:2 NKJV

There are some of your graces that would never be discovered if it were not for your trials. Do you not know that your faith never looks so grand in summer as it does in winter? Love is too often like a glowworm, showing little light except in the midst of darkness. Hope is like a star—not to be seen in the sunshine of prosperity and only to be discovered in the night of adversity. Afflictions are often the black foils in which God sets the jewels of His children's graces to make them shine better.

A little while ago, you were on your knees saying, "Lord, I fear I have no faith: Let me know that I have faith." Was not this really, though perhaps unconsciously, praying for trials? For how can you know that you have faith until your faith is exercised? God often sends us trials so that our graces may be discovered and that we may be assured of their existence.

Besides, it is not merely discovery; growth in grace is the result of sanctified trials. God often takes away our comforts and our privileges in order to make us better Christians. May this not account for the troubles that you are passing through? Is not the Lord bringing out your graces and making them grow?

THE GOD OF ALL COMFORT

God, that comforteth those that are cast down. . . .

2 CORINTHIANS 7:6 KJV

Who comforts like Him? Go to some poor, melancholy, distressed child of God; tell him sweet promises and whisper in his ear words of comfort. Comfort him as you may, it will be only a note or two of mournful resignation that you will get from him; you will bring forth no psalms of praise, no hallelujahs, no joyful sonnets. But let God come to His child, let Him lift up his countenance, and the mourner's eyes glisten with hope.

You could not have cheered him, but the Lord has done it: "He is the God of all comfort." It is marvelous how one sweet word of God will make whole songs for Christians. One word of God is like a piece of gold, and the Christian is the gold beater and can hammer that promise out for whole weeks. So, Christian, you need not sit down in despair. Go to the Comforter, and ask Him to give you consolation.

You are a poor, dry well. You have heard it said that when a pump is dry, you must pour water down it first, and then you will get water; and so, Christian, when you are dry, go to God, ask Him to shed abroad His joy in your heart, and then your joy shall be full. Do not go to earthly acquaintances, for you will find them Job's comforters after all; but go first and foremost to your "God who comforteth those who are cast down," and you will soon say, "In the multitude of my thoughts within me, Your comforts delight my soul."

DWELL IN SAFETY

If you make the Most High your dwelling. . .
then no harm will befall you.

PSALM 91:9–10 NIV

The Israelites in the wilderness were continually exposed to change. Whenever the pillar halted its motion, the tents were pitched; but tomorrow, before the morning sun had risen, the trumpet sounded, the ark was in motion, and the fiery, cloudy pillar was leading the way through the narrow defiles of the mountain, up the hillside, or along the arid waste of the wilderness. Yet they had an abiding home in their God, His cloudy pillar, and its flame by night.

They must go onward from place to place, continually changing, never having time to settle and to say, "Now we are secure; in this place we shall dwell." "Yet," says Moses, "though we are always changing, Lord, You have been our dwelling place throughout all generations."

The Christian knows no change with regard to God. He may be rich today and poor tomorrow, he may be sickly today and well tomorrow, he may be in happiness today, tomorrow he may be distressed—but there is no change with regard to his relationship to God. If He loved me yesterday, He loves me today. My unmoving mansion of rest is my blessed Lord.

Let prospects be ruined, let hopes be blasted, let joy be withered, let mildews destroy everything; I have lost nothing of what I have in God. He is "my strong habitation where unto I can continually resort." I am a pilgrim in the world but at home in my God. In the earth I wander, but in God I dwell in a quiet habitation.

PRECIOUS JESUS

He is precious.

1 PETER 2:7 KJV

Peter tells us that Jesus is precious; but he did not and could not tell us how precious, nor could any of us compute the value of God's unspeakable gift. Words cannot set forth the preciousness of the Lord Jesus to His people nor fully tell how essential He is to their satisfaction and happiness.

Believer, have you not found in the midst of plenty a sore famine if your Lord has been absent? The sun was shining, but Christ had hidden Himself; and all the world was black to you—or it was night, and since the bright and morning star was gone, no other star could yield you so much as a ray of light. What a howling wilderness is this world without our Lord! If once He hid Himself from us, withered are the flowers of our garden, our pleasant fruits decay, the birds suspend their songs, and a tempest overturns our hopes. All earth's candles cannot make daylight if the Sun of Righteousness is eclipsed. He is the soul of our soul, the light of our light, the life of our life.

Dear reader, what would you do in the world without Him, when you wake up and look forward to the day's battle? What would you do at night, when you come home jaded and weary, if there were no door of fellowship between you and Christ? Blessed be His name, He will not suffer us to try our lot without Him for Jesus never forsakes His own. Yet let the thought of what life would be without Him enhance His preciousness.

COMFORT IN AFFLICTION

I have chosen *thee* in the furnace of affliction.

ISAIAH 48:10 KJV

Let affliction come—God has chosen me. Poverty, you may enter my door, but God is in the house already; and He has chosen me. Sickness, you may intrude, but I have a balsam ready—God has chosen me. Whatever befalls me in this vale of tears, I know that He has "chosen" me.

If, believer, you require still greater comfort, remember that you have the Son of Man with you in the furnace. In that silent chamber of yours, there sits by your side One whom you have not seen but whom you love; and often when you know it not, He makes all your bed in your affliction and smoothes your pillow for you. You are in poverty, but in that lonely house of yours, the Lord of life and glory is a frequent visitor. He loves to come into these desolate places that He may visit you. Your friend sticks closely to you. You cannot see Him, but you may feel the pressure of His hands.

Do you not hear His voice? Even in the valley of the shadow of death, He says, "Fear not, I am with you; be not dismayed for I am your God." Fear not, Christian; Jesus is with you. In all your fiery trials, His presence is both your comfort and safety. He will never leave one whom He has chosen for His own. "Fear not for I am with you" is His sure Word of promise to His chosen ones in the "furnace of affliction."

GRACE WITHOUT LIMIT

"My grace is sufficient for you."

2 CORINTHIANS 12:9 NKJV

If none of God's saints were poor and tried, we should not know half so well the consolations of divine grace. When we find the wanderer who does not have a place to lay his head, who yet can say, "Still will I trust in the Lord"; when we see the pauper starving on bread and water, who still glories in Jesus; when we see the bereaved widow overwhelmed in affliction, and yet having faith in Christ, oh, what honor it reflects on the Gospel. God's grace is illustrated and magnified in the poverty and trials of believers.

Saints bear up under every discouragement, believing that all things work together for their good and that out of apparent evils a real blessing shall ultimately spring—that their God will either work a deliverance for them speedily or most assuredly support them in the trouble, as long as He is pleased to keep them in it. This patience of the saints proves the power of divine grace.

He who would glorify his God must set his account upon meeting with many trials. No man can be illustrious before the Lord unless his conflicts are many. If then yours is a much-tried path, rejoice in it because you will better show forth the all-sufficient grace of God. As for His failing you, never dream of it—hate the thought. The God who has been sufficient until now should be trusted to the end.

My Salvation

Say unto my soul, I am thy salvation.

PSALM 35:3 KJV

David had his doubts; for why should he pray, "Say unto my soul, I am your salvation," if he did not sometimes have doubts and fears? "I am not the only saint who has to complain of weakness of faith." If David doubted, I need not conclude that I am no Christian because I have doubts. The text reminds me that David was not content while he had doubts and fears; but he went at once to the mercy seat to pray for assurance, for he valued it as much as fine gold. I, too, must labor after an abiding sense of my acceptance in the Beloved.

David knew where to obtain full assurance. He went to God in prayer. I must be alone with God if I would have a clear sense of Jesus' love. Let my prayers cease, and my eye of faith will grow dim. Much in prayer, much in heaven; slow in prayer, slow in progress.

David would not be satisfied unless his assurance had a divine source. Nothing short of a divine testimony in the soul will ever content the true Christian. Moreover, David could not rest unless his assurance had a vivid personality about it.

"Lord, if You should say this to all the saints, it were nothing unless You should say it to me. I have sinned, I deserve not Your smile, I scarcely dare to ask it; but oh, say to my soul, even to my soul, 'I am your salvation.' Let me have a present, personal, infallible, indisputable sense that I am Yours and that You are mine."

SOUGHT OUT

Thou shalt be called, Sought out.

ISAIAH 62:12 KJV

The surpassing grace of God is seen very clearly in that we were not only sought, but also sought out. Men seek for a thing that is lost upon the floor of the house, but in such a case there is only seeking, not seeking out. The loss is more perplexing and the search more persevering when a thing is sought out.

Glory be to unconquerable grace, we were sought out! No gloom could hide us, no filthiness could conceal us; we were found and brought home. Glory be to infinite love, God the Holy Spirit restored us! The lives of some of God's people, if they could be written, would fill us with holy astonishment. Strange and marvelous are the ways that God used in their case to find His own. Blessed be His name, He never relinquishes the search until the chosen are sought out effectually.

They are not a people sought today and cast away tomorrow. Almightiness and wisdom combined will make no failures; they shall be called "Sought out"! That any should be sought out is matchless grace, but that we should be sought out is grace beyond degree! We can find no reason for it but God's own sovereign love and can only lift up our heart in wonder and praise the Lord that this night we wear the name of "Sought out."

Neighborly Love

"You shall love your neighbor."

Matthew 5:43 nasb

"Love your neighbor." Perhaps he rolls in riches and you are poor. God has given him these gifts; covet not his wealth, and think no evil thoughts concerning him. Be content with your own lot if you cannot improve it, but do not look upon your neighbor and wish that he were as yourself. Love him, and then you will not envy him.

Perhaps you are rich and near you reside the poor. Do not resist calling them neighbor. You are bound to love them. The world calls them your inferiors. In what are they inferior? They are far more your equals than your inferiors. You are by no means better than they. They are men, and what are you more than that? Take heed that you love your neighbor even though he is in rags or sunken in the depths of poverty.

But perhaps you say, "I cannot love my neighbors, because for all I do, they return ingratitude and contempt." So much the more room for the heroism of love. He who dares the most shall win the most; and if rough be your path of love, tread it boldly, still loving your neighbors through thick and thin. Heap coals of fire on their heads, and if they be hard to please, seek not to please them but to please your Master; and remember if they spurn your love, your Master has not spurned it; and your deed is as acceptable to Him as if it had been acceptable to them.

Love your neighbor, for in so doing, you are following the footsteps of Christ.

Be Diligent and Prosper

He did it with all his heart, and *prospered.*

2 Chronicles 31:21 KJV

It is the general rule of the moral universe that those men prosper who do their work with all their hearts, while those are almost certain to fail who go to their labor leaving half their hearts behind them. God is not pleased to send wealth to those who will not dig in the field to find its hidden treasure. It is universally confessed that if a man would prosper, He must be diligent in business.

It is the same in religion as it is in other things. If you would prosper in your work for Jesus, let it be heart work and let it be done with all your heart. Put as much force, energy, heartiness, and earnestness into religion as you do into business, for it deserves far more. The Holy Spirit helps our infirmities, but He does not encourage our idleness; He loves active believers.

Wholeheartedness shows itself in perseverance; there may be failure at first, but the earnest worker will say, "It is the Lord's work, and it must be done; my Lord has bidden me do it, and in His strength I will accomplish it."

Christian, are you "with all your heart" serving your Master? Remember the earnestness of Jesus! Think what heart work was His! When He sweat great drops of blood, it was no light burden He had to carry upon those blessed shoulders; and when He poured out His heart, it was no weak effort He was making for the salvation of His people. Was Jesus in earnest, and are we lukewarm?

GO TO THE CROSS

Let us *search* and *try* our ways,
and *turn* again to the LORD.

LAMENTATIONS 3:40 KJV

The spouse who fondly loves her absent husband longs for his return; an extended separation is a semideath to her spirit. And so with souls who love the Savior greatly, they must see His face; they cannot bear that He should be away and no more hold communion with them.

A reproaching glance, an uplifted finger will be grievous to loving children who fear to offend their tender father and are only happy in His smile. It was so once with you. A scripture, a threatening, a touch of the rod of affliction, and you went to your Father's feet, crying, "Show me wherefore You contendest with me?"

Is it so now? Are you content to follow Jesus from a distance? Can you contemplate suspended communion with Christ? Can you bear to have your Beloved walking contrary to you because you walk contrary to Him? Have your sins separated you and your God? Let me affectionately warn you, for it is a grievous thing when we can live contentedly without the present enjoyment of the Savior's face.

No matter how hard, how insensible, how dead we may have become, let us go again in all the rags and poverty and defilement of our natural condition. Let us clasp that cross, let us look into those languid eyes, let us bathe in that fountain filled with blood—this will bring back to us our first love; this will restore the simplicity of our faith and the tenderness of our heart.

His Wounds Removed Our Sin

By *his* wounds we are *healed*.

Isaiah 53:5 niv

Pilate delivered our Lord to the lictors to be scourged. The Roman scourge was a most dreadful instrument of torture. It was made of the sinews of oxen, and sharp bones were intertwined among the sinews; so that every time the lash came down, these pieces of bone inflicted fearful laceration and tore off the flesh from the bone. The Savior was, no doubt, bound to the column and thus beaten. He had been beaten before; but this of the Roman lictors was probably the most severe of His scourgings.

My soul, stand here and weep over His poor stricken body. Believer, can you gaze upon Him without tears as He stands before you, the mirror of agonizing love? He is at once fair as the lily for innocence and red as the rose with the crimson of His own blood. As we feel the sure and blessed healing that His stripes have wrought in us, does not our heart melt at once with love and grief? If ever we have loved our Lord Jesus, surely we must feel that affection glowing now within our bosoms.

We would be compelled to go to our chambers and weep, but since our business calls us away, we will first pray our Beloved to print the image of His bleeding self upon the tablets of our hearts all the day; and at nightfall we will return to commune with Him and sorrow that our sin should have cost Him so dearly.

HUMILITY

Before honor comes humility.

PROVERBS 15:33 NASB

Humiliation of soul always brings a positive blessing with it. If we empty our hearts of self, God will fill them with His love. Stoop if you would climb to heaven. You must grow downward that you may grow upward; for the sweetest fellowship with heaven is to be had by humble souls, and by them alone. God will deny no blessing to a thoroughly humbled spirit. "Blessed are the poor in spirit, for theirs is the kingdom of heaven" with all its riches and treasures.

God blesses us all up to the full measure and extremity of what it is safe for Him to do. If you do not get a blessing, it is because it is not safe for you to have one. If our heavenly Father were to let your unhumbled spirit win a victory in His holy war, you would pilfer the crown for yourself; and meeting with a fresh enemy, you would fall a victim, so that you are kept low for your own safety.

When a man is sincerely humble and never ventures to touch so much as a grain of the praise, there is scarcely any limit to what God will do for him. Humility makes us ready to be blessed by the God of all grace and fits us to deal efficiently with our fellowmen. True humility is a flower that will adorn any garden. Whether it is prayer or praise, whether it is work or suffering, the genuine salt of humility cannot be used in excess.

A Prayer of Repentance

Deliver me from bloodguiltiness, O *God,*
thou God of my salvation: and my tongue
shall sing aloud of *thy* righteousness.

Psalm 5'1:14 KJV

In this solemn confession, observe that David plainly names his sin. He does not call it manslaughter nor speak of it as an imprudence by which an unfortunate accident occurred to a worthy man, but he calls it by its true name: bloodguiltiness. He did not actually kill the husband of Bathsheba; but still it was planned in David's heart that Uriah should be slain, and he was before the Lord his murderer.

Learn in confession to be honest with God. Do not give fair names to foul sins; call them what you will, they will smell no sweeter. What God sees them to be, that do you labor to feel them to be; and with all openness of heart, acknowledge their real character. Observe that David was evidently oppressed with the heinousness of his sin.

It is easy to use words, but it is difficult to feel their meaning. The fifty-first Psalm is the photograph of a contrite spirit. Let us seek after like brokenness of heart; for however excellent our words may be, if our heart is not conscious of the hell-deservingness of sin, we cannot expect to find forgiveness.

The psalmist ends with a commendable vow: If God will deliver him, he will "sing aloud." Who can sing in any other style of such a mercy as this! But note the subject of the song— "thy righteousness." We must sing of the finished work of a precious Savior, and he who knows most of forgiving love will sing the loudest.

FORGIVE MY SINS

Look on my affliction and my pain,
and forgive all my sins.

PSALM 25:18 NKJV

It is good for us when prayers about our sorrows are linked with pleas concerning our sins—when, being under God's hand, we are not wholly taken up with our pain but remember our offenses against God. It is good, also, to take both sorrow and sin to the same place. It was to God that David carried his sorrow; it was to God that David confessed his sin. Even your little sorrows you may turn over to God, for He counts the hairs of your head; and your great sorrows you may commit to Him, for He holds the ocean in the hollow of His hand. Go to Him, whatever your present trouble, and you will find Him able and willing to relieve you.

But we must take our sins to God, too. We must carry them to the cross, that the blood may fall upon them, to purge away their guilt.

We are to go to the Lord with sorrows and with sins in the right spirit. David cries, "Lord, as for my affliction and my pain, I will not dictate to Your wisdom. I will leave them to You; I would be glad if my pain were removed, but do as You will. As for my sins, Lord, I know what I want with them; I must have them forgiven—I cannot endure to lie under their curse for a moment." A Christian counts sorrow lighter in the scale than sin; he can bear that his troubles should continue, but he cannot support the burden of his transgressions.

THE BLOOD OF CHRIST

The precious blood of Christ. . .

4 PETER 1:19 NIV

Standing at the foot of the cross, we see hands and feet and side, all pouring forth crimson streams of Precious Blood. It is "precious" because of its redeeming and atoning efficacy. By it the sins of Christ's people are atoned for; they are redeemed from under the law—they are reconciled to God, made one with Him.

Christ's blood is also "precious" in its cleansing power; it "cleans from all sin." "Though your sins be as scarlet, they shall be as white as snow." Through Jesus' blood there is not a spot left upon any believer; no wrinkle nor any such thing remains. Oh, Precious Blood that makes us clean, removing the stains of abundant iniquity and permitting us to stand accepted in the Beloved, notwithstanding the many ways in which we have rebelled against our God.

The blood of Christ is likewise "precious" in its preserving power. We are safe from the destroying angel under the sprinkled blood. Remember it is God's seeing the blood that is the true reason for our being spared. Here is comfort for us when the eye of faith is dim, for God's eye is still the same.

The blood of Christ is "precious" also in its sanctifying influence. The same blood that justifies by taking away sin quickens the new nature and leads it onward to subdue sin and to follow out the commands of God. There is no motive for holiness so great as that which streams from the veins of Jesus.

DEATH DEFEATED

That through death He might destroy
him who had the power of death. . .

HEBREWS 2:14 NKJV

Oh, child of God, death has lost its sting because the devil's power over it is destroyed. Then cease to fear dying. Ask grace from God the Holy Spirit, that by an intimate knowledge and a firm belief of your Redeemer's death, you may be strengthened for that hour. Living near the cross of Calvary, you may think of death with pleasure and welcome it when it comes with intense delight. It is sweet to die in the Lord: It is a covenant blessing to sleep in Jesus.

Death is no longer banishment; it is a return from exile, a going home to the many mansions where the loved ones already dwell. The distance between glorified spirits in heaven and militant saints on earth seems great, but it is not so. We are not far from home—a moment will bring us there. "Absent from the body, present with the Lord." Think not that a long period intervenes between the instant of death and the eternity of glory. When the eyes close on earth, they open in heaven.

Then, child of God, what is there for you to fear in death, seeing that through the death of your Lord its curse and sting are destroyed?

CALM IN THE MIDST OF TERROR

You shall not be afraid
of the terror by night.

PSALM 91:5 NKJV

What is this terror? It may be the cry of fire or the noise of thieves or the shriek of sudden sickness or death. We live in the world of death and sorrow. This should not alarm us, for be the terror what it may, the promise is that the believer shall not be afraid. Why should he? God our Father is here and will be here all through the lonely hours; He is an almighty Watcher, a sleepless Guardian, a faithful Friend. Nothing can happen without His direction, for even hell itself is under His control. Darkness is not dark to Him. He has promised to be a wall of fire around His people—and who can break through such a barrier?

Worldlings might be afraid, for they have an angry God above them, a guilty conscience within them, and a yawning hell beneath them; but we who rest in Jesus are saved from all these through rich mercy.

If we give way to foolish fear, we lead others to doubt the reality of godliness. We ought to be afraid of being afraid, lest we should displease the Holy Spirit by foolish distrust. God has not forgotten to be gracious nor shut up His tender mercies; it may be night in the soul, but there need be no terror, for the God of love changes not. Children of light may walk in darkness, but they are not therefore cast away; no, they are now enabled to prove their adoption by trusting in their heavenly Father as hypocrites cannot do.

More Than Conquerors

In all these things we are more than conquerors
through him who loved us.

Romans 8:37 niv

We go to Christ for forgiveness and then too often look to the law for power to fight our sins. Take your sins to Christ's cross, for the old man can only be crucified there: We are crucified with Him. The only weapon to fight sin with is the spear that pierced the side of Jesus.

To give an illustration: You want to overcome an angry temper; how do you begin? It is very possible you have never tried the right way of going to Jesus with it. How did I get salvation? I came to Jesus just as I was, and I trusted Him to save me. I must kill my angry temper in the same way. It is the only way in which I can ever kill it. I must go to the cross with it and say to Jesus, "Lord, I trust You to deliver me from it."

Are you covetous? Do you feel the world entangle you? You may struggle against this evil as long as you wish, but if it is your besetting sin, you will never be delivered from it in any way but by the blood of Jesus.

Take it to Christ. Tell Him: "Lord, I have trusted You, and Your name is Jesus, for You save Your people from their sins. Lord, this is one of my sins; save me from it!" You must be conquerors through Him who has loved you, if conquerors at all.

CALL ON GOD

God, even our own *God*. . .

PSALM 67:6 KJV

It is strange how little use we make of the spiritual blessings that God gives us, but it is stranger still how little use we make of God Himself. Though He is "our own God," we apply ourselves but little to Him and ask but little of Him. How seldom do we ask counsel at the hands of the Lord! How often do we go about our business without seeking His guidance! In our troubles how constantly do we strive to bear our burdens ourselves, instead of casting them upon the Lord that He may sustain us!

This is not because we may not, for the Lord seems to say, "I am yours, soul, come and make use of Me as you will; you may freely come to My store, and the oftener the more welcome." It is our own fault if we make not free with the riches of our God. Then since you have such a friend and He invites you, draw from Him daily. Never want while you have a God to go to, never fear or faint while you have God to help you, go to your treasure and take whatever you need—there is all that you could want.

Make use of Him in prayer. Go to Him often because He is your God. Use Him constantly by faith at all times. Whatever you are and wherever you are, remember God is just what you want and just where you want, and that He can do all you want.

PROMISES OF SCRIPTURE

Remember the word unto *thy* servant,
upon which *thou* hast caused me to hope.

PSALM 119:49 KJV

Whatever your special need may be, you may readily find some promise in the Bible suited to it. Are you faint and feeble because your way is rough and you are weary? Here is the promise: "He gives power to the faint." When you read such a promise, take it back to the great Promiser and ask Him to fulfill His own Word.

Are you seeking after Christ and thirsting for closer communion with Him? This promise shines like a star upon you: "Blessed are they who hunger and thirst after righteousness, for they shall be filled." Take that promise to the throne continually; do not plead anything else, but go to God over and over again with this: "Lord, You have said it, do as You have said."

Are you distressed because of sin and burdened with the heavy load of your iniquities? Listen to these words: "I, even I, am He who blots out your transgressions and will no more remember your sins." You have no merit of your own to plead why He should pardon you, but plead His written engagements and He will perform them.

If you have lost the sweet sense of the Savior's presence and are seeking Him with a sorrowful heart, remember the promises: "Return unto Me, and I will return unto you"; "For a small moment have I forsaken you, but with great mercies will I gather you."

My Refuge

You are my refuge in the day of disaster.

Jeremiah 17:17 NIV

The path of the Christian is not always bright with sunshine; he has his seasons of darkness and of storm. At certain periods clouds cover the believer's sun, and he walks in darkness and sees no light.

There are many who have rejoiced in the presence of God for a season, they have basked in the sunshine in the earlier stages of their Christian career, they have walked along the "green pastures" by the side of the "still waters," but suddenly they find the glorious sky is clouded; instead of the land of Goshen, they have to tread the sandy desert; in the place of sweet waters, they find troubled streams, bitter to their taste; and they say, "Surely if I were a child of God, this would not happen."

Oh, do not say that, you who are walking in darkness. The best of God's saints must drink the bitterness; the dearest of His children must bear the cross. No Christian has enjoyed perpetual prosperity; no believer can always keep his harp from the willows. Perhaps the Lord allotted you at first a smooth and unclouded path because you were weak and timid. He tempered the wind to the shorn lamb, but now that you are stronger in the spiritual life, you must enter upon the riper and rougher experience of God's full-grown children.

We need winds and tempests to exercise our faith, to tear off the rotten bough of self-dependence, and to root us more firmly in Christ. The day of evil reveals to us the value of our glorious hope.

GOD'S PLEASURE IN HIS CHILDREN

The LORD takes pleasure in His people.

PSALM 149:4 NKJV

How comprehensive is the love of Jesus! There is no part of His people's interests that He does not consider, and there is nothing that concerns their welfare that is not important to Him. Not merely does He think of you, believer, as an immortal being but as a mortal being, too. Do not deny it or doubt it: "The very hairs of your head are all numbered." "The steps of a good man are ordered by the Lord, and he delights in His way." Believer, rest assured that the heart of Jesus cares about your common affairs.

The breadth of His tender love is such that you may resort to Him in all matters; for in all your afflictions, He is afflicted, and like as a father pities his children, so does He pity you. Oh, what a heart is His that does not merely comprehend the persons of His people, but comprehends also the diverse and innumerable concerns of all those persons!

Do you think that you can measure the love of Christ? Think of what His love has brought you—justification, adoption, sanctification, eternal life! The riches of His goodness are unsearchable; you shall never be able to tell them out or even conceive them. Oh, the breadth of the love of Christ! Go to your rest rejoicing, for thou art no desolate wanderer but a beloved child, watched over, cared for, supplied, and defended by your Lord.

WISDOM AND TRUST

He that *handleth* a matter wisely shall find good:
and whoso *trusteth* in the Lord, happy is he.

PROVERBS 16:20 KJV

Wisdom is man's true strength, and under its guidance, he best accomplishes the ends of his being. Wisely handling the matter of life gives to man the richest enjoyment and presents the noblest occupation for his powers; hence by it he finds good in the fullest sense.

Wisdom is the compass by which man is to steer across the trackless waste of life; without it he is a derelict vessel, the sport of winds and waves. A man must be prudent in such a world as this, or he will find no good but be betrayed into unnumbered ills. If, trained by the Great Teacher, we follow where He leads, we shall find good, even while in this dark abode.

But where shall this wisdom be found? Many have dreamed of it but have not possessed it. Where shall we learn it? Let us listen to the voice of the Lord, for He has declared the secret; He has revealed to the sons of men where true wisdom lies, and we have it in the text, "Whoso trusteth in the Lord, happy is he." The true way to handle a matter wisely is to trust in the Lord.

This is the sure clue to the most intricate labyrinths of life; follow it and find eternal bliss. He who trusts in the Lord has a diploma for wisdom granted by inspiration: Happy is he now, and happier shall he be above. Lord, teach me the wisdom of faith.

Waiting with Patience

All the days of my
appointed time will I wait.

Job 14:14 KJV

A little stay on earth will make heaven more heavenly. Nothing makes rest so sweet as toil; nothing renders security so pleasant as exposure to alarms. Our battered armor and scarred countenances will render more illustrious our victory above, when we are welcomed to the seats of those who have overcome the world.

We should not have full fellowship with Christ if we did not for a while sojourn below, for He was baptized with a baptism of suffering among men, and we must be baptized with the same if we would share His kingdom. Fellowship with Christ is so honorable that the sorest sorrow is a light price by which to procure it.

Another reason for our lingering here is for the good of others. We would not wish to enter heaven until our work is done, and it may be that we are yet ordained to minister to souls lost in the wilderness of sin. Our prolonged stay here is doubtless for God's glory.

A tried saint, like a well-cut diamond, glitters much in the King's crown. We are God's workmanship, in whom He will be glorified by our afflictions. Our time is fixed and settled by eternal decree. Let us not be anxious about it, but wait with patience until the gates of pearl shall open.

THE RISEN CHRIST

But now *Christ* has been
raised from the dead.

1 CORINTHIANS 15:20 NASB

The whole system of Christianity rests upon the fact that "Christ is risen from the dead"; for "If Christ be not risen, then is our preaching vain and your faith is also vain: You are yet in your sins." The divinity of Christ finds its surest proof in His resurrection. It would not be unreasonable to doubt His Deity if He had not risen.

Moreover, Christ's sovereignty depends upon His resurrection, "For to this end Christ died and rose and revived, that He might be Lord both of the dead and the living." Again our justification, that choice blessing of the covenant, is linked with Christ's triumphant victory over death and the grave. Further, our very regeneration is connected with His resurrection, for we are "begotten again unto a lively hope by the resurrection of Jesus Christ from the dead."

And most certainly our ultimate resurrection rests here, for "If the Spirit of Him who raised up Jesus from the dead dwell in you, He who raised up Christ from the dead shall also quicken your mortal bodies by His Spirit which dwells in you." If Christ is not risen, then we shall not rise; but if He is risen, then they who are asleep in Christ have not perished, but in their flesh shall surely behold their God.

Thus the silver thread of resurrection runs through all the believer's blessings, from his regeneration onward to his eternal glory, and binds them together. How important then will this glorious fact be in his estimation, and how will he rejoice that beyond a doubt it is established, that "now is Christ risen from the dead."

Joy Follows Pain

Weeping may endure for a night,
but joy *cometh* in the morning.

Psalm 30:5 KJV

If you are in a night of trial, think of tomorrow; cheer your heart with the thought of the coming of the Lord. Be patient, for "He comes with clouds descending." Be patient! The Husbandman waits until He reaps His harvest. Be patient, for you know who has said, "Behold, I come quickly, and my reward is with me, to give to every man according as his work shall be."

Your head may be crowned with thorny troubles now, but it shall wear a starry crown before long; your hand may be filled with cares—it shall sweep the strings of the harp of heaven soon. Your garments may be soiled with dust now; they shall be white in a short time.

Wait a little longer. How despicable our troubles and trials will seem when we look back upon them! Looking at them presently, they seem immense; but when we get to heaven, we shall then "with transporting joys recount the labors of our feet." Our trials will then seem light and momentary afflictions. Let us go on boldly; after the dark of night the morning comes, which is more than they can say who are shut up in the darkness of hell.

Do you know what it is to live in the future—to live on expectation—to antedate heaven? It may be dark now, but it will soon be light; it may be all trial now, but it will soon be all happiness. What does it matter if "weeping may endure for a night," when "joy comes in the morning"?

Afterward

Afterward it *yieldeth* the peaceable fruit.

Hebrews 12:11 KJV

How happy are tried Christians afterward. There is no calm more deep than that which succeeds a storm. Who has not rejoiced in clear skies after rain? Our sorrows, like the passing keels of the vessels upon the sea, leave a silver line of holy light behind them "afterward." It is peace—sweet, deep peace—which follows the horrible turmoil that once reigned in our tormented, guilty souls.

The Christian has his best things last, and he therefore in this world receives his worst things first. But even his worst things are "afterward" good things. Even now he grows rich by his losses, he rises by his falls, he lives by dying and becomes full by being emptied; if then his grievous afflictions yield him so much peaceable fruit in this life, what shall be the full vintage of joy "afterward" in heaven?

If his dark nights are as bright as the world's days, what shall his days be? If even his starlight is more splendid than the sun, what must his sunlight be? If he can sing in a dungeon, how sweetly will he sing in heaven? If he can praise the Lord in the fires, how will he extol Him before the eternal throne? If evil be good to him now, what will the overflowing goodness of God be to him then?

Who would not choose to be a Christian? Who would not bear the present cross for the crown that comes afterward? Wait, dear soul, and let patience have her perfect work.

A Purpose Fulfilled

The LORD will fulfill his purpose for me.

PSALM 138:8 NIV

The confidence that the psalmist expressed was a divine confidence. His dependence was on the Lord alone. The psalmist was wise; he rested upon nothing short of the Lord's work. It is the Lord who has begun the good work within us; it is He who has carried it on, and if He does not finish it, it never will be complete. If there be one stitch in the celestial garment of our righteousness that we are to insert ourselves, then we are lost; but this is our confidence: The Lord who began will perfect. He has done it all, must do it all, and will do it all.

Our confidence must not be in what we have done nor in what we have resolved to do, but entirely in what the Lord will do. Unbelief insinuates: "You will never be able to stand. Look at the evil of your heart; you can never conquer sin. Remember the sinful pleasures and temptations of the world that beset you; you will be certainly allured by them and led astray."

Yes, we should indeed perish if left to our own strength. But thanks be to God, He will perfect that which concerns us and bring us to the desired haven. We can never be too confident when we confide in Him alone and never too much concerned to have such a trust.

SHARE CHRIST WITH ZEAL

Be zealous.

REVELATION 3:19 KJV

If you would see souls converted, if you would place crowns upon the head of the Savior, and His throne lifted high, then be filled with zeal. Every grace will have accomplishments, but this will be first; prudence, knowledge, patience, and courage will follow in their places, but zeal must lead the van. This zeal is the fruit of the Holy Spirit: It draws its vital force from the continued operations of the Holy Spirit in the soul.

If our inner life dwindles, if our heart beats slowly before God, we shall not know zeal; but if all be strong and vigorous within, then we cannot but feel a loving anxiety to see the kingdom of Christ come and His will done on earth, even as it is in heaven. A deep sense of gratitude will nourish Christian zeal. We find abundant reason why we should spend and be spent for God.

And zeal is also stimulated by the thought of the eternal future. It looks with tearful eyes down to the flames of hell, and it cannot slumber: It looks up with anxious gaze to the glories of heaven, and it cannot but bestir itself. It feels that time is short compared with the work to be done, and therefore it devotes all that it has to the cause of its Lord.

And it is ever strengthened by the remembrance of Christ's example. Let us prove that we are His disciples by manifesting the same spirit of zeal.

GREAT THINGS

The *Lord* hath done great things for us;
whereof we are glad.

PSALM 126:3 KJV

Some Christians are prone to look on the dark side of everything and to dwell more upon what they have gone through
than upon what God has done for them. Ask for their im-
pression of the Christian life, and they will describe their
continual conflicts, their deep afflictions, their sad adversi-
ties, and the sinfulness of their hearts, yet with scarcely any
allusion to the mercy and help that God has granted them.

But a Christian whose soul is in a healthy state will come
forward joyously and say, "I will speak not about myself but
to the honor of my God. He has brought me up out of a horrible pit and out of the miry clay and set my feet upon a rock
and established my goings; and He has put a new song in my
mouth, even praise unto our God. The Lord has done great
things for me, whereof I am glad."

It is true that we endure trials, but it is just as true that we
are delivered out of them. It is true that we have our corrup-
tions, and mournfully we know this; but it is quite as true that
we have an all-sufficient Savior who overcomes these corrup-
tions and delivers us from their dominion.

The deeper our troubles, the louder our thanks to God
who has led us through and preserved us. Our griefs cannot mar the melody of our praise; we reckon them to be the
bass part of our life's song: "He has done great things for us,
whereof we are glad."

EXPLORE GOD'S WORD

Search the scriptures.

JOHN 5:39 KJV

The Greek word here rendered "search" signifies a strict, close, diligent, curious search, such as men make when they are seeking gold, or hunters when they are in earnest after game. We must not rest content with having given a superficial reading to a chapter or two, but with the candle of the Spirit, we must deliberately seek out the hidden meaning of the Word. Holy scripture requires searching—much of it can only be learned by careful study. There is milk for babes but also meat for strong men.

No man who merely skims the book of God can profit from it; we must dig and mine until we obtain the hidden treasure. The door of the Word only opens to the key of diligence. The scriptures claim searching. They are the writings of God—who shall dare to treat them with levity? He who despises them despises the God who wrote them. God forbid that any of us should leave our Bibles to become swift witnesses against us in the great day of account. The Word of God will repay searching. Scripture grows upon the student. It is full of surprises.

The scriptures reveal Jesus: "They are they which testify of Me." No more powerful motive can be urged upon Bible readers than this: He who finds Jesus finds life, heaven, all things. Happy is he who, searching his Bible, discovers his Savior.

A HOLY CALLING

Who has saved us and called
us with a holy calling. . .

2 TIMOTHY 1:9 NKJV

Believers in Christ Jesus are saved. They are not looked upon as persons who are in a hopeful state and may ultimately be saved, but they are already saved. Salvation is not a blessing to be enjoyed upon the deathbed and to be sung of in a future state above, but a matter to be obtained, received, promised, and enjoyed now. The Christian is saved in God's purpose; God has ordained him unto salvation, and that purpose is complete.

This complete salvation is accompanied by a holy calling. Those whom the Savior saved are in due time effectually called by the power of God unto holiness: They leave their sins; they endeavor to be like Christ; they choose holiness, not out of any compulsion but of a new nature that leads them to rejoice in holiness just as naturally as before they delighted in sin. God neither chose them nor called them because they were holy, but He called them that they might be holy.

The excellencies that we see in a believer are as much the work of God as the atonement itself. Thus is brought out very sweetly the fullness of the grace of God. Salvation must be of grace because the Lord is the author of it, and what motive but grace could move Him to save the guilty? Salvation must be of grace because the Lord works in such a manner that our righteousness is forever excluded. Such is the believer's privilege—a present salvation; such is the evidence that he is called to it—a holy life.

PERMANENCE IN CHRIST

The things which cannot
be shaken may remain.

HEBREWS 12:27 NKJV

Whatever your losses have been or may be, you enjoy present salvation. You are standing at the foot of His cross, trusting alone in the merit of Jesus' precious blood, and no rise or fall of the markets can interfere with your salvation in Him; no breaking of banks, no failures and bankruptcies can touch that. Then you are a child of God. God is your Father. No change of circumstances can ever rob you of that.

Although by losses brought to poverty and stripped bare, you can say, "He is my Father still. In my Father's house are many mansions; therefore will I not be troubled." You have another permanent blessing, namely, the love of Jesus Christ. He who is God and man loves you with all the strength of His affectionate nature—nothing can affect that. The fig tree may not blossom, and the flocks may cease from the field; it matters not to the man who can sing, "My Beloved is mine, and I am His." Our best portion and richest heritage we cannot lose.

Whatever troubles come, let us act as men; let us show that we are not such little children as to be cast down by what may happen in this poor fleeting state of time. Our country is Immanuel's land, our hope is above the sky and therefore calm as the summer's ocean; we will see the wreck of everything earthborn and yet rejoice in the God of our salvation.

PROPER SERVICE

Let every man abide in the same
calling wherein he was called.

4 CORINTHIANS 7:20 KJV

Beloved, it is not office, it is earnestness; it is not position, it is grace that will enable us to glorify God. God is most surely glorified in that cobbler's stall, where the godly worker, as he plies the awl, sings of the Savior's love. The name of Jesus is glorified by the poor, unlearned carter as he drives his horse and blesses his God or speaks to his fellow laborer by the roadside, as much as by the popular divine who throughout the country is thundering out the Gospel.

God is glorified by our serving Him in our proper vocations. Take care that you do not forsake the path of duty by leaving your occupation, and take care you do not dishonor your profession while in it. Think little of yourselves, but do not think too little of your callings. Every lawful trade may be sanctified by the Gospel to noblest ends. Turn to the Bible, and you will find the most menial forms of labor connected either with most daring deeds of faith or with persons whose lives have been illustrious for holiness.

Therefore be not discontented with your calling. Whatever God has made your position or your work, abide in that unless you are quite sure that He calls you to something else. Let your first care be to glorify God to the utmost of your power where you are. Fill your present sphere to His praise, and if He needs you in another, He will show it to you. Lay aside vexatious ambition, and embrace peaceful content.

KEEP YOUR EYES ON JESUS

Let us fix our eyes on Jesus.

HEBREWS 12:2 NIV

It is the Holy Spirit's constant work to turn our eyes away from self to Jesus; but Satan's work is just the opposite of this, for he is constantly trying to make us regard ourselves instead of Christ. He insinuates: "Your sins are too great for pardon, you have no faith, you do not repent enough, you will never be able to endure, you have not the joy of His children, you have a wavering hold of Jesus." All these are thoughts about self, and we shall never find comfort or assurance by looking within.

But the Holy Spirit turns our eyes entirely away from self: He tells us that we are nothing, but that "Christ is all in all." It is not your hold of Christ that saves you—it is Christ; it is not your joy in Christ that saves you—it is Christ; it is not even faith in Christ, though that be the instrument—it is Christ's blood and merits; therefore, look not to your hope, but to Jesus, the source of your hope; look not to your faith, but to Jesus, the author and finisher of your faith.

It is what Jesus is, not what we are, that gives rest to the soul. Keep your eye simply on Him; let His death, His sufferings, His merits, His glories, His intercession be fresh upon your mind; when you wake in the morning, look to Him; when you lie down at night, look to Him. Do not let your hopes or fears come between you and Jesus; follow Him, and He will never fail you.

HEARTS OF GLADNESS

In *him* our hearts *rejoice,*
for we *trust* in *his* holy name.

PSALM 33:24 NIV

Christians can rejoice even in the deepest distress. Although trouble may surround them, they still sing; and, like many birds, they sing best in their cages. The waves may roll over them, but their souls soon rise to the surface and see the light of God's countenance. Trouble does not necessarily bring consolation with it to the believer, but the presence of the Son of God in the fiery furnace with him fills his heart with joy.

He is sick and suffering, but Jesus visits him and makes his bed for him. He is dying, but Jesus puts His arms around him and cries, "Fear not, beloved, to die is to be blessed; the waters of death have their fountainhead in heaven. They are not bitter; they are sweet as nectar, for they flow from the throne of God." As the departing saint wades through the stream and the billows gather around him, the same voice sounds in his ears, "Fear not, I am with thee; be not dismayed, I am your God."

As he nears the borders of the infinite unknown, Jesus says, "Fear not, it is your Father's good pleasure to give you the kingdom." Thus strengthened and consoled, the believer is not afraid to die; no, he is even willing to depart, for since he has seen Jesus as the morning star, he longs to gaze upon Him as the sun in his strength. Truly the presence of Jesus is all the heaven we desire.

AWAITING INSTRUCTION

Lead me in *thy* truth, and *teach* me: for *thou art*
the *God* of my salvation; on *thee* do I *wait* all the day.

PSALM 25:5 KJV

When the believer has begun with trembling feet to walk in the way of the Lord, he asks to be still led onward like a little child upheld by its parent's helping hand, and he craves to be further instructed in the alphabet of truth. Jehovah is the Author and Perfecter of salvation to His people. Reader, is He the God of your salvation? Do you find in the Father's election, in the Son's atonement, and in the Spirit's quickening all the grounds of your eternal hopes?

If so, you may use this as an argument for obtaining further blessings; if the Lord has ordained to save you, surely He will not refuse to instruct you in His ways. It is a happy thing when we can address the Lord with the confidence that David here manifests; it gives us great power in prayer and comfort in trial. "On you do I wait all the day."

Patience is the fair handmaid and daughter of faith; we cheerfully wait when we are certain that we shall not wait in vain. It is our duty and our privilege to wait upon the Lord in service, in worship, in expectancy, in trust all the days of our life. Our faith will be tried faith, and if it is of the true kind, it will bear continued trial without yielding. We shall not grow weary of waiting upon God if we remember how long and how graciously He once waited for us.

God Is for Us

When I *cry* unto *thee*, then shall mine enemies
turn back: this I know; for God is for me.

PSALM 56:9 KJV

It is impossible for any human speech to express the full meaning of this delightful phrase: "God is for me." He was "for us" before the worlds were made; He was "for us," or He would not have given His well-beloved Son; He was "for us" when He smote the Only Begotten and laid the full weight of His wrath upon Him—He was "for us" though He was against Him; He was "for us" when we were ruined in the fall—He loved us notwithstanding all; He was "for us" when we were rebels against Him and with a high hand were bidding Him defiance; He was "for us," or He would not have brought us humbly to seek His face.

He has been "for us" in many struggles; we have been summoned to encounter hosts of dangers, we have been assailed by temptations from without and within—how could we have remained unharmed to this hour if He had not been "for us"? He is "for us" with all the infinity of His being, with all the omnipotence of His love, with all the infallibility of His wisdom; arrayed in all His divine attributes, He is "for us"—eternally and immutably "for us," "for us" when yonder blue skies shall be rolled up like a worn-out vesture, "for us" throughout eternity.

And because He is "for us," the voice of prayer will always ensure His help.

THE GLORY OF GOD

The LORD our God has shown us his glory.

DEUTERONOMY 5:24 NIV

God's great design in all His works is the manifestation of His own glory. Any aim less than this would be unworthy of Himself. But how shall the glory of God be manifested to such fallen creatures as we are?

Self must stand out of the way that there may be room for God to be exalted; and this is the reason why He often brings His people into difficulties: That being made conscious of their own folly and weakness, they may be fitted to behold the majesty of God when He comes forth to work their deliverance.

He whose life is one even and smooth path will see but little of the glory of the Lord, for he has few occasions of self-emptying and little fitness for being filled with the revelation of God. They who navigate little streams and shallow creeks know but little of the God of tempests; but they who "do business in great waters," these see His "wonders in the deep." Among the huge waves of bereavement, poverty, temptation, and reproach, we learn the power of Jehovah because we feel the littleness of man.

Thank God then if you have been led by a rough road. It is this that has given you your experience of God's greatness and loving-kindness. Your troubles have enriched you with a wealth of knowledge to be gained by no other means: Your trials have been the cleft of the rock in which Jehovah has set you that you might behold His glory as it passed by.

Our Inheritance in Christ

The earnest of our inheritance. . .

Ephesians 1:14 KJV

What enlightenment, what joys, what consolation, what delight of heart is experienced by that man who has learned to feed on Jesus, and on Jesus alone. Yet the realization that we have of Christ's preciousness is, in this life, imperfect at the best. We have tasted "that the Lord is gracious," but we do not yet know how good and gracious He is, although what we know of His sweetness makes us long for more.

We are but beginners now in spiritual education: For although we have learned the first letters of the alphabet, we cannot read words yet, much less can we put sentences together; but as one says, "He who has been in heaven but five minutes knows more than the general assembly of divines on earth." We have many ungratified desires at present, but soon every wish will be satisfied; and all our powers shall find the sweetest employment in that eternal world of joy.

Oh, Christian, within a very little time you will be rid of all your trials and your troubles. Your eyes now suffused with tears will weep no longer. You will gaze in ineffable rapture upon the splendor of Him who sits upon the throne. Even more, upon His throne you will sit. The triumph of His glory you will share; His crown, His joy, His paradise, these will be yours, and you will be coheir with Him who is the heir of all things.

A Witness of Joy

They. . . *rejoiced*: for *God* had
made them rejoice with great joy.

Nehemiah 12:43 KJV

They "rejoiced: for God had made them rejoice with great joy." It was not all singing and giving. When the wheels of the machine are well oiled, the whole machine goes easily; and when the man has the oil of joy, then in his business and in his family, the wheels of his nature glide along sweetly and harmoniously because he is a glad and a happy man.

Oh, happy households where the joy is not confined to one but where all partake of it! Too many need all the religion they can get to cheer their own hearts, and their poor families and neighbors sit shivering in the cold of ungodliness. Be like those well-constructed stoves of our own houses that send out all the heat into the room.

Send out the heat of piety into your house, and let all the neighbors participate in the blessing, for so the text finishes: "The joy of Jerusalem was heard even afar off." The joy of the Lord should be observed throughout our neighborhood, and many who might otherwise have been careless of true religion will then inquire, "What makes these people glad and creates such happy households?" Your joy shall thus be God's missionary.

REMEMBER GOD'S PROMISES

Exceedingly great and precious promises. . .

2 PETER 1:4 NKJV

If you would know experimentally the preciousness of the promises and enjoy them in your own heart, meditate upon them. Thinking over the hallowed words will often be the prelude to their fulfillment. While you are considering them, the blessing that you are seeking will insensibly come to you. Many a Christian who has thirsted for the promise has found the favor that it ensured gently distilling into his soul even while he has been considering the divine record; and he has rejoiced that he was led to lay the promise near his heart.

But besides meditating upon the promises, seek to receive them as being the very words of God. My soul, it is God, even your God, God who cannot lie, who speaks to you. This Word of His that you are now considering is as true as His own existence. He is a God unchangeable. He has not altered a word that has gone out of His mouth, nor called back one single consolatory sentence. Nor does He lack any power; it is the God who made the heavens and the earth who has spoken. Nor can He fail in wisdom as to the time when He will bestow the favors, for He knows when it is best to give and when better to withhold.

Therefore, seeing that it is the Word of a God so true, so immutable, so powerful, so wise, I will and must believe the promise. If we thus meditate upon the promises and consider the Promiser, we shall experience their sweetness and obtain their fulfillment.

CONTINUALLY WITH YOU

Nevertheless I am continually with *You*.

PSALM 73:23 NKJV

"Nevertheless"—as if, notwithstanding all the foolishness and ignorance that David had just been confessing to God, not one atom the less was it true and certain that David was saved and accepted, and that the blessing of being constantly in God's presence was undoubtedly his. Fully conscious of his own lost estate and of the deceitfulness and vileness of his nature, yet by a glorious outburst of faith, he sings, "Nevertheless I am continually with thee."

Believer, endeavor in like spirit to say, "Nevertheless, since I belong to Christ, I am continually with God!" By this is meant continually upon His mind; He is always thinking of me for my good. Continually before His eye—the eye of the Lord never sleeps but is perpetually watching over my welfare. Continually in His hand—so that none will be able to pluck me out from it. Continually on His heart—worn there as a memorial, even as the high priest bore the names of the twelve tribes upon His heart forever.

"You always think of me, O God. You are always making providence work for my good. You have set me as a signet upon Your arm. Your love is strong as death; many waters cannot quench it, neither can the floods drown it. You see me in Christ, and though in myself despised, You behold me as wearing Christ's garments and washed in His blood; and thus I stand accepted in Your presence. I am thus continually in Your favor—'continually with You.'"

THE STRENGTH OF SPIRITUAL KNOWLEDGE

The people that do know
their *God* shall be strong.

DANIEL 11:32 KJV

Every believer understands that to know God is the highest and best form of knowledge; and this spiritual knowledge is a source of strength to the Christian. It strengthens his faith. Believers are constantly spoken of in the scriptures as being persons who are enlightened and taught of the Lord; they are said to "have an unction from the Holy One," and it is the Spirit's peculiar office to lead them into all truth, and all this for the increase and the fostering of their faith.

Knowledge strengthens love, as well as faith. Knowledge opens the door, and then through that door we see our Savior. If we know but little of the excellences of Jesus, what He has done for us and what He is doing now, we cannot love Him much; but the more we know Him, the more we shall love Him. Knowledge also strengthens hope. How can we hope for a thing if we do not know of its existence?

Knowledge supplies us reasons for patience. How shall we have patience unless we know something of the sympathy of Christ and understand the good that is to come out of the correction that our heavenly Father sends us? Nor is there one single grace of the Christian that, under God, will not be fostered and brought to perfection by holy knowledge. How important then it is that we should grow not only in grace but also in the "knowledge" of our Lord and Savior Jesus Christ.

ALL THINGS WORK TOGETHER FOR GOOD

We *know* that all things work together
for good to them that *love God*.

ROMANS 8:28 KJV

Upon some points a believer is absolutely sure. He knows, for instance, that God sits in the stern sheets of the vessel when it rocks most. He believes that an invisible hand is always on the world's rudder, and that wherever providence may drift, Jehovah steers it. That reassuring knowledge prepares Him for everything.

He knows that God is always wise, and knowing this he is confident that there can be no accidents, no mistakes—that nothing can occur that ought not to arise. He can say, "If I should lose all I have, it is better that I should lose than have if God so wills: The worst calamity is the wisest and the kindest thing that could befall me if God ordains it."

"We know that all things work together for good to them who love God." The Christian does not merely hold this as a theory, but he knows it as a matter of fact. Everything has worked for good as yet. Every event as yet has worked out the most divinely blessed results; and so believing that God rules all, that He governs wisely, that He brings good out of evil, the believer's heart is assured, and he is enabled calmly to meet each trial as it comes.

The believer can in the spirit of true resignation pray, "Send me what You will, my God, as long as it comes from You; there has never come an ill portion from Your table to any of Your children."

OUR EVERLASTING CONSOLATION

Everlasting consolation. . .

2 THESSALONIANS 2:16 KJV

"Everlasting consolation"—here is the most excellent of all, for the eternity of comfort is the crown and glory of it. What is this "everlasting consolation"? It includes a sense of pardoned sin. A Christian has received in his heart the witness of the Spirit that his iniquities are put away like a cloud, and his transgressions like a thick cloud. If sin is pardoned, is not that an everlasting consolation?

Next, the Lord gives His people an abiding sense of acceptance in Christ. The Christian knows that God looks upon him as standing in union with Jesus. Union to the risen Lord is a consolation of the most abiding order; it is in fact everlasting. Let sickness prostrate us; have we not seen hundreds of believers as happy in the weakness of disease as they would have been in blooming health? Let death's arrows pierce us to the heart; our comfort does not die, for have not we often heard the songs of saints as they have rejoiced because the living love of God was shed abroad in their hearts in dying moments? Yes, a sense of acceptance in the Beloved is an everlasting consolation.

Moreover, the Christian has a conviction of his security. God has promised to save those who trust in Christ: The Christian does trust in Christ, and he believes that God will be as good as His Word and will save him. He feels that he is safe by virtue of his being bound up with the person and work of Jesus.

SHEEP PRAISING THEIR SHEPHERD

He shall *stand* and *feed* in
the strength of the *Lord*.

MICAH 5:4 KJV

Christ's reign in His Church is that of a shepherd-king. He has supremacy, but it is the superiority of a wise and tender shepherd over his needy and loving flock; He commands and receives obedience, but it is the willing obedience of the well-cared-for sheep, rendered joyfully to their beloved Shepherd whose voice they know so well. He rules by the force of love and the energy of goodness.

His reign is practical in its character. The great Head of the Church is actively engaged in providing for His people. He does not sit down upon the throne in empty state or hold a scepter without wielding it in government. No, He stands and feeds.

His reign is continual in its duration. His eyes never slumber, and His hands never rest; His heart never ceases to beat with love, and His shoulders are never weary of carrying His people's burdens.

His reign is effectually powerful in its action. Wherever Christ is, there is God; and whatever Christ does is the act of the Most High. It is a joyful truth to consider that He who stands today representing the interests of His people is very God of very God to whom every knee shall bow. Happy are we who belong to such a Shepherd, whose humanity communes with us and whose divinity protects us. Let us worship and bow down before Him as the people of His pasture.

RECEIVING THROUGH GIVING

He who refreshes others
will himself be refreshed.

PROVERBS 11:25 NIV

To get, we must give; to accumulate, we must scatter; to make ourselves happy, we must make others happy; and in order to become spiritually vigorous, we must seek the spiritual good of others. In watering others, we are ourselves watered.

How? Our efforts to be useful bring out our powers for usefulness. We have latent talents and dormant faculties that are brought to light by exercise. Our strength for labor is hidden even from ourselves, until we venture forth to fight the Lord's battles or to climb the mountains of difficulty. We often find in attempting to teach others that we gain instruction for ourselves. Oh, what gracious lessons some of us have learned at sickbeds! We went to teach the scriptures; we came away blushing that we knew so little of them.

In our conversation with poor saints, we are taught the way of God more perfectly for ourselves and get a deeper insight into divine truth—so that watering others makes us humble. We discover how much grace there is where we had not looked for it and how much the poor saint may surpass us in knowledge. Our own comfort is also increased by our working for others. We endeavor to cheer them, and the consolation gladdens our own heart.

Like the two men in the snow—one chafed the other's limbs to keep him from dying and in so doing kept his own blood in circulation and saved his own life. Give then, and it shall be given unto you, good measure, pressed down, and running over.

NO MORE GRIEF

The voice of weeping shall
no longer be heard.

ISAIAH 65:19 NKJV

The glorified weep no more, for all outward causes of grief are gone. There are no broken friendships in heaven. Poverty, famine, peril, persecution, and slander are unknown there. No pain distresses; no thought of death or bereavement saddens. They weep no more for they are perfectly sanctified. They are without fault before His throne and are fully conformed to His image. Well may they cease to mourn who have ceased to sin. They weep no more because all fear of change is past.

They know that they are eternally secure. Sin is shut out, and they are shut in. Countless cycles may revolve, but eternity shall not be exhausted; and while eternity endures, their immortality and blessedness shall coexist with it. They are forever with the Lord. They weep no more because every desire is fulfilled. They cannot wish for anything that they have not in possession.

Eye and ear, heart and hand, judgment, imagination, hope, desire, will, all the faculties are completely satisfied; and imperfect as our present ideas are of the things that God has prepared for them who love Him, yet we know enough by the revelation of the Spirit that the saints above are supremely blessed. The joy of Christ, which is an infinite fullness of delight, is in them. That same joyful rest remains for us. It may not be far distant. "Wherefore comfort one another with these words."

Hope for the Barren

"Sing, O barren!"

ISAIAH 54:1 NKJV

There are times when we feel very barren. Prayer is lifeless, love is cold, faith is weak; each grace in the garden of our heart languishes and droops. In such a condition, what are we to do?

I can sing of Jesus Christ. I can talk of visits that the Redeemer has paid to me. I can magnify the great love with which He loved His people when He came from the heights of heaven for their redemption. I will go to the cross again. Come, my soul, heavy laden you once were and lost your burden there. Go to Calvary again. Perhaps that very cross that gave you life may give you fruitfulness.

What is my barrenness? It is the platform for His fruit-creating power. What is my desolation? It is the setting for the sapphire of His everlasting love. I will go in poverty, I will go in helplessness, I will go in all my shame and backsliding; I will tell Him that I am still His child, and in confidence in His faithful heart, I will sing and cry aloud.

Sing, believer, for it will cheer your heart and the hearts of other desolate ones. Sing on, for now that you are really ashamed of being barren, you will be fruitful soon; now that God makes you reluctant to be without fruit, He will soon cover you with clusters. The experience of our barrenness is painful, but the Lord's visitations are delightful. A sense of our own poverty drives us to Christ, and that is where we need to be, for in Him is our fruit found.

SIMPLY WAIT

Wait on the *LORD*.

PSALM 27:14 KJV

There are hours of perplexity when the most willing spirit, anxiously desirous to serve the Lord, does not know which direction to take. Then what should it do? Fly back in cowardice, turn to the right hand in fear, or rush forward in presumption?

No, simply wait. Wait in prayer, however. Call upon God and tell Him your difficulty and plead His promise of aid. In dilemmas between one duty and another, wait with simplicity of soul upon the Lord. It is sure to be well with us when we feel and know our own folly and are heartily willing to be guided by the will of God. But wait in faith. Express your unwavering confidence in Him; for unfaithful, untrusting waiting is but an insult to the Lord. Believe that He will come at the right time. Wait in quiet patience, not rebelling because you are under the affliction but blessing your God for it.

Accept the case as it is, and put it as it stands, simply and with your whole heart, without any self-will, into the hand of your covenant God, saying, "Now, Lord, not my will but Yours be done. I do not know what to do; I am brought to extremities, but I will wait until You cleave the floods or drive back my foes. I will wait if You keep me many a day, for my heart is fixed upon You alone, O God; and my spirit waits for You in the full conviction that You will yet be my joy and my salvation, my refuge and my strong tower."

TRUST YOURSELF TO GOD

On *mine* arm shall they trust.

ISAIAH 54:5 KJV

In seasons of severe trial, the Christian has nothing on earth that he can trust in and is therefore compelled to cast himself on his God alone. When no human deliverance can avail, he must simply and entirely trust himself to the providence and care of God.

There is no confiding in God sometimes because of the multitude of our friends; but when a man is so poor, so friend-less, so helpless that he has nowhere else to turn, he flies into his Father's arms and is blessedly clasped within them! When he is burdened with troubles so pressing that he cannot tell them to any but his God, he may be thankful for them for he will learn more of his Lord than at any other time.

Now that You have only God to trust in, see that you place your full confidence in Him. Do not dishonor the Lord by unworthy doubts and fears, but be strong in faith, giving glory to God. Now is the time for feats of faith and valiant exploits. Be strong and very courageous, and the Lord your God shall certainly, as surely as He built the heavens and the earth, glorify Himself in your weakness and magnify His might in the midst of your distress. Your faith would lose its glory if it rested on anything discernible by the carnal eye. May the Holy Spirit give you rest in Jesus.

TRIALS OF THE RIGHTEOUS

The LORD trieth the righteous.

PSALM 11:5 KJV

All events are under the control of Providence; consequently all the trials of our outward life are traceable at once to the great First Cause. All providences are doors to trial. Even our mercies, like roses, have their thorns. Men may be drowned in seas of prosperity as well as in rivers of affliction. Our mountains are not too high and our valleys are not too low for temptations: Trials lurk on all roads. We are beset and surrounded with dangers.

Yet no shower falls from the threatening cloud without permission; every drop has its order before it hastens to the earth. The trials that come from God are sent to prove and strengthen our graces, and so at once to illustrate the power of divine grace, to test the genuineness of our virtues, and to add to their energy. You would never have possessed the precious faith that now supports you if the trial of your faith had not been like unto fire.

Worldly ease is a great foe to faith; it loosens the joints of holy valor and snaps the sinews of sacred courage. While the wheat sleeps comfortably in the husk, it is useless to man; it must be threshed out of its resting place before its value can be known. Thus it is well that Jehovah tries the righteous, for it causes them to grow rich toward God.

Bad News? Don't Fear

He will not be afraid of evil tidings.

PSALM 112:7 NKJV

Christian, you ought not to dread the arrival of evil tidings; because if you are distressed by them, how do you differ from other men? Other men have not your God to fly to; they have never proved His faithfulness as you have done, and it is no wonder if they are bowed down with alarm and cowed with fear. But you profess to be of another spirit; you have been begotten again unto a lively hope, and your heart lives in heaven and not on earthly things. Now if you are seen to be distracted as other men, what is the value of that grace that you profess to have received? Where is the dignity of that new nature that you claim to possess?

If you should be filled with alarm, you would doubtless be led into the sins so common to others under trying circumstances. The ungodly, when they are overtaken by evil tidings, rebel against God; they murmur and think that God deals harshly with them. Will you fall into that same sin? Will you provoke the Lord as they do?

Moreover, unconverted men often run to wrong means in order to escape from difficulties, and you will be sure to do the same if your mind yields to the present pressure. Trust in the Lord, and wait patiently for Him. Your wisest course is to do as Moses did at the Red Sea: "Stand still, and see the salvation of God."

ENCOURAGE FELLOW CHRISTIANS

"Encourage him."

DEUTERONOMY 1:38 NASB

God employs His people to encourage one another. He did not say to an angel, "Gabriel, my servant Joshua is about to lead my people into Canaan—go, encourage him." God never works needless miracles; if His purposes can be accomplished by ordinary means, He will not use miraculous agency. Gabriel would not have been half so well fitted for the work as Moses. A brother's sympathy is more precious than an angel's embassy.

The angel, swift of wing, had better known the Master's bidding than the people's temper. An angel had never experienced the hardness of the road nor seen the fiery serpents, nor had he led the stiff-necked multitude in the wilderness as Moses had done. We should be glad that God usually works for man by man. It forms a bond of brotherhood, and being mutually dependent on one another, we are fused more completely into one family. Labor to help others; especially strive to encourage them.

Leave the young believer to discover the roughness of the road by degrees, but tell him of the strength that dwells in God, of the sureness of the promise, and of the charms of communion with Christ. Aim to comfort the sorrowful and to animate the desponding. Speak a word in season to him who is weary, and encourage those who are fearful to go on their way with gladness.

God encourages you by His promises, Christ encourages you as He points to the heaven He has won for you, and the Spirit encourages you as He works in you to will and to do of His own will and pleasure.

GOD'S GIFTS

For this child I *prayed*.

1 SAMUEL 1:27 KJV

Devout souls delight to look upon those mercies that they have obtained in answer to supplication, for they can see God's especial love in them. When we can name our blessings Samuel, that is, "asked of God," they will be as dear to us as her child was to Hannah. Peninnah had many children, but they came as common blessings unsought in prayer; Hannah's one heaven-given child was dearer by far because he was the fruit of earnest pleadings.

Did we pray for the conversion of our children? How doubly sweet when they are saved to see in them our own petitions fulfilled! Better to rejoice over them as the fruit of our pleadings than as the fruit of our bodies.

Have we sought of the Lord some choice spiritual gift? When it comes to us, it will be wrapped up in the gold cloth of God's faithfulness and truth, and so be doubly precious.

Have we petitioned for success in the Lord's work? How joyful is the prosperity that comes flying upon the wings of prayer!

Even when prayer speeds not, the blessings grow all the richer for the delay. That which we win by prayer, we should dedicate to God, as Hannah dedicated Samuel. The gift came from heaven; let it go to heaven. Prayer brought it, gratitude sang over it, let devotion consecrate it.

GOD REJOICES IN US;
WE REJOICE IN GOD

I will rejoice over them to do them good.

JEREMIAH 32:41 KJV

How heart-cheering to the believer is the delight that God has in His saints! We cannot see any reason in ourselves why the Lord should take pleasure in us; we cannot take delight in ourselves, for we often have to groan being burdened, conscious of our sinfulness and deploring our unfaithfulness—and we fear that God's people cannot take much delight in us, for they must perceive so much of our imperfections and our follies that they may rather lament our infirmities than admire our graces.

But we love to dwell upon this transcendent truth, this glorious mystery: that as the bridegroom rejoices over the bride, so does the Lord rejoice over us. In what strong language He expresses His delight in His people! Who could have conceived of the Eternal One as bursting forth into a song? Yet it is written, "He will rejoice over you with joy, He will rest in His love, He will joy over you with singing."

As He looked upon the world He had made, He said, "It is very good"; but when He beheld those who are the purchase of Jesus' blood, His own chosen ones, it seemed as if the great heart of the Infinite could restrain itself no longer but overflowed in divine exclamations of joy. Should we not utter our grateful response to such a marvelous declaration of His love, and sing, "I will rejoice in the Lord; I will joy in the God of my salvation"?

ACCEPTED IN CHRIST

Blessed *be* the *God* and *Father* of our *Lord Jesus Christ*,
who hath blessed us with all spiritual blessings in heavenly places
in *Christ*: . . .To the praise of the
glory of *his* grace, wherein *he* hath made us
accepted in the beloved.

EPHESIANS 1:3, 6 KJV

What a state of privilege! It includes our justification before God, but the term "acceptance" in the Greek means more than that. It signifies that we are the objects of divine complacence—even of divine delight. How marvelous that we mortals, sinners, should be the objects of divine love! But it is only "in the beloved."

Rejoice then, believer, in this: "There is nothing acceptable here!" But look at Christ, and see if there is not everything acceptable there. Your sins trouble you; but God has cast your sins behind His back, and you are accepted in the Righteous One. You have to fight with corruption and to wrestle with temptation, but you are already accepted in Him who has overcome the powers of evil. The devil tempts you; be of good cheer: He cannot destroy you for you are accepted in Him who has broken Satan's head.

Know by full assurance your glorious standing. Even glorified souls are not more accepted than you are. They are only accepted in heaven "in the beloved," and you are even now accepted in Christ after the same manner.

THE VIEW FROM GOD'S THRONE

The *LORD looks* from heaven;
He sees all the sons of men.

PSALM 33:13 NKJV

Perhaps no figure of speech represents God in a more gracious light than when He is spoken of as stooping from His throne and coming down from heaven to attend to the wants and to behold the woes of mankind. We cannot help pouring out our heart in affection for our Lord who inclines His ear from the highest glory and puts it to the lip of the dying sinner whose failing heart longs after reconciliation. How can we but love Him when we know that He numbers the very hairs of our heads, marks our paths, and orders our ways?

Especially is this great truth brought near to our heart when we recollect how attentive He is, not merely to the temporal interests of His creatures but to their spiritual concerns. Though leagues of distance lie between the finite creature and the infinite Creator, yet there are links uniting both. When a tear is wept by you, do not think that God does not behold; for "Like as a father pities his children, so the Lord pities them who fear Him." Your sigh is able to move the heart of Jehovah, your whisper can incline His ear unto you, your prayer can stay His hand, your faith can move His arm.

Do not think that God sits on high taking no account of you. For the eyes of the Lord run to and fro throughout the whole earth to show Himself strong on behalf of those whose heart is perfect toward Him.

Praise God Daily

Sing the glory of his name;
make his praise glorious!

PSALM 66:2 NIV

It is not left to our own option whether we shall praise God or not. Praise is God's most righteous due, and every Christian, as the recipient of His grace, is bound to praise God from day to day. It is true we have no commandment prescribing certain hours of song and thanksgiving: But the law written upon the heart teaches us that it is right to praise God. Yes, it is the Christian's duty to praise God. It is not only a pleasurable exercise, but it is the absolute obligation of his life.

You who are always mourning, do not think that you are guiltless in this respect or imagine that you can discharge your duty to your God without songs of praise. You are bound by the bonds of His love to bless His name as long as you live, and His praise should continually be in your mouth, for you are blessed in order that you may bless Him. If you do not praise God, you are not bringing forth the fruit that He, as the divine Husbandman, has a right to expect at your hands.

Arise and chant His praise. With every morning's dawn, lift up your notes of thanksgiving, and let every setting sun be followed with your song. Girdle the earth with your praises; surround it with an atmosphere of melody, and God Himself will hearken from heaven and accept your music.

FUTURE FAULTLESSNESS

Faultless before the presence of *his* glory. . .

JUDE 1:24 KJV

Revolve in your mind that wondrous word "faultless"! We are far off from it now; but as our Lord never stops short of perfection in His work of love, we shall reach it one day. The Savior who will keep His people to the end will also present them at last to Himself as "a glorious Church, not having spot or wrinkle or any such thing, but holy and without blemish."

All the jewels in the Savior's crown are without a single flaw. All the maids of honor who attend the Lamb's wife are pure virgins without spot or stain. But how will Jesus make us faultless? He will wash us from our sins in His own blood until we are white and fair as God's purest angel; and we shall be clothed in His righteousness, that righteousness that makes the saint who wears it positively faultless, perfect in the sight of God.

The work of the Holy Spirit within us will be altogether complete. He will make us so perfectly holy that we shall have no lingering tendency to sin. We shall be holy even as God is holy, and in His presence we shall dwell forever. Saints will not be out of place in heaven; their beauty will be as great as that of the place prepared for them. Sin gone, Satan shut out, temptation past forever, and ourselves "faultless" before God, this will be heaven indeed!

THE IMPORTANCE OF PRAYER

We *lift* up our heart and
hands toward *God* in heaven.

LAMENTATIONS 3:41 NASB

The act of prayer teaches us our unworthiness, which is a very salutary lesson for such proud beings as we are. If God gave us favors without constraining us to pray for them, we should never know how poor we are, but a true prayer is an inventory of wants, a catalogue of necessities, a revelation of hidden poverty. While it is an application to divine wealth, it is a confession of human emptiness.

The most healthy state of a Christian is to be always empty in self and constantly depending upon the Lord for supplies, to be always poor in self and rich in Jesus. Prayer is in itself, apart from the answer that it brings, a great benefit to the Christian. As the runner gains strength for the race by daily exercise, so for the great race of life, we acquire energy by the hallowed labor of prayer. An earnest pleader comes out of his closet, even as the sun rises from the chambers of the east, rejoicing like a strong man to run his race.

Prayer girds human weakness with divine strength, turns human folly into heavenly wisdom, and gives to troubled mortals the peace of God. We know not what prayer cannot do! We thank You, great God, for the mercy seat, a choice proof of Your marvelous loving-kindness. Help us to use it in the right manner throughout this day!

Spiritual Renewal

Renew a right spirit within me.

Psalm 51:10 KJV

A backslider, if there be a spark of life left in him, will groan after restoration. In this renewal the same exercise of grace is required as at our conversion. We needed repentance then; we certainly need it now. We wanted faith that we might come to Christ at first; only the like grace can bring us to Jesus now. We wanted a word from the Most High, a word from the lips of the loving One to end our fears then; we shall soon discover, when under a sense of present sin, that we need it now.

No man can be renewed without as real and true a manifestation of the Holy Spirit's energy as he felt at first, because the work is as great, and flesh and blood are as much in the way now as ever they were. Let your personal weakness be an argument to make you pray earnestly to God for help. Oh, that you may have grace to plead with God, as though you pleaded for your very life—"Lord, renew a right spirit within me."

He who sincerely prays to God to do this will prove his honesty by using the means through which God works. Be much in prayer, live much upon the Word of God, be careful to watch over the future uprisings of sin. Continue in all those blessed ordinances that will foster and nourish your dying graces; and knowing that all the power must proceed from Him, cease not to cry, "Renew a right spirit within me."

ACKNOWLEDGING OUR WEAKNESS

"For my power is made perfect in weakness."

2 CORINTHIANS 12:9 NIV

A primary qualification for serving God with any amount of success, and for doing God's work well and triumphantly, is a sense of our own weakness. When God's warrior marches forth to battle strong in his own might, when he boasts, "I know that I shall conquer; my own right arm and my conquering sword shall get unto me the victory," defeat is not far distant. God will not go forth with that man who marches in his own strength.

Those who serve God must serve Him in His own way and in His strength, or He will never accept their service. That which man does unaided by divine strength God can never own. The mere fruits of the earth He casts away; He will only reap that corn, the seed of which was sown from heaven, watered by grace, and ripened by the sun of divine love. God will empty out all that you have before He will put His own into you. The river of God is full of water, but not one drop of it flows from earthly springs. God will have no strength used in His battles but the strength that He Himself imparts.

Are you mourning over your own weakness? Take courage, for there must be a consciousness of weakness before the Lord will give you victory. Your emptiness is but the preparation for your being filled, and your casting down is but the making ready for your lifting up.

WATER FOR THE THIRSTY

*I will pour water upon
him that is thirsty.*

ISAIAH 44:3 KJV

When a believer has fallen into a low, sad state of feeling, he often tries to lift himself out of it by chastening himself with dark and doleful fears. Such is not the way to rise from the dust but to continue in it. It is not the law, but the Gospel that saves the seeking soul at first; and it is not a legal bondage, but Gospel liberty that can restore the fainting believer afterward. Slavish fear does not bring the backslider back to God, but the sweet wooings of love allure him to Jesus' bosom.

Are you this morning thirsting for the living God and unhappy because you cannot find Him to the delight of your heart? Have you lost the joy of religion, and is this your prayer: "Restore unto me the joy of Your salvation"? Are you conscious also that you are barren, like the dry ground, that you are not bringing forth the fruit unto God that He has a right to expect of you?

Then here is exactly the promise that you need: "I will pour water upon him who is thirsty." You shall receive the grace you so much require, and you shall have it to the utmost reach of your needs. Water refreshes the thirsty: You shall be refreshed; your desires shall be gratified. Your life shall be quickened by fresh grace. Whatever good quality there is in divine grace, you shall enjoy it to the full; all the riches of divine grace you shall receive in plenty.

GRAVEN ON HIS PALMS

Behold, I have graven thee
upon the palms of *my* hands.

ISAIAH 49:16 KJV

No doubt a part of the wonder that is concentrated in the word "Behold" is excited by the unbelieving lamentation of the preceding sentence. Zion said, "The Lord has forsaken me, and my God has forgotten me." How amazed the divine mind seems to be at this wicked unbelief! What can be more astounding than the unfounded doubts and fears of God's favored people?

The Lord's loving word of rebuke should make us blush; He cries, "How can I have forgotten thee when I have graven you upon the palms of My hands?" We do not know which to wonder most at: the faithfulness of God or the unbelief of His people. He keeps His promise a thousand times, and yet the next trial makes us doubt Him. He never fails, and yet we are as continually vexed with anxieties, molested with suspicions, and disturbed with fears.

"Behold" is a word intended to excite admiration. Here, indeed, we have a theme for marveling. Heaven and earth may well be astonished that rebels should obtain so great a nearness to the heart of infinite love as to be written upon the palms of His hands. The name is there, but that is not all: "I have graven your person, your image, your case, your circumstances, your sins, your temptations, your weaknesses, your wants, your works: I have graven you, everything about you, all that concerns you; I have put you altogether there."

Will you ever say again that God has forsaken you when He has graven you upon His own palms?

PONDER GOD'S GOODNESS

But Mary *kept* all these things,
and *pondered* them in her heart.

LUKE 2:19 KJV

There was an exercise on the part of this blessed woman of three powers of her being: her memory—she kept all these things; her affection—she kept them in her heart; her intellect—she pondered them. Memory, affection, and understanding were all exercised in relation to the things that she had heard. Beloved, remember what you have heard of your Lord Jesus and what He has done for you. Let your memory treasure up everything about Christ that you have either felt or known or believed, and then let your fond affections hold Him fast forevermore. Love the person of your Lord!

Let your intellect be exercised concerning the Lord Jesus. Meditate on what you read: Stop not at the surface; dive into the depths. Abide with your Lord: Let Him not be to you as a wayfaring man who lingers for a night, but constrain Him, saying, "Abide with us, for the day is far spent." Hold Him, and do not let Him go.

The word "ponder" means "to weigh." Make ready the balances of judgment. Oh, but where are the scales that can weigh the Lord Christ? "He takes up the isles as a very little thing"; who shall take Him up? "He weighs the mountains in scales"; in what scales shall we weigh Him? If your understanding cannot comprehend, let your affections apprehend; and if your spirit cannot compass the Lord Jesus in the grasp of understanding, let it embrace Him in the arms of affection.

A Benediction of Peace

Peace *I leave* with you,
my peace *I give* unto you.

John 14:27 KJV

Beloved friends, as you go to your families, as you go through life, as you go into eternity, I pray that you "go in peace." It is heaven here on earth to possess "the peace of God which passeth all understanding." Peace should be the continual portion of all believers.

This is what the angels sang when our Lord Jesus appeared on earth: "Glory to God in the highest, and on earth peace, goodwill toward men." And as it was at the beginning of our Savior's life, it was also at the end, for this was our Lord's legacy to all His disciples: "Peace I leave with you, my peace I give unto you." He who is called "the God of peace" should be very precious to your soul.

Peace is the result of what the Savior has done for you. Has He forgiven you? Then you have peace. Has He saved you? Then feel an inward peace that no one can take from you! Did He die for you? Then you can never die in the full meaning of the word. Has He risen for you? Then because He lives, you will live, also; so do not let your heart be troubled, but be at peace. Will He come again to receive you to Himself? Then let your peace be like a river flowing from the very throne of God!

Scripture Index